Laughter

LAUGHTER

A Theological Essay

Karl-Josef Kuschel

SCM PRESS LTD

Translated by John Bowden from the German
Lachen. Gottes und des Menschen Kunst
published 1994 by Herder Verlag, Freiburg im Breisgau.

0 334 00867 0

First British edition published 1994
by SCM Press Ltd,
26-30 Tottenham Road, London N1 4BZ

Phototypeset by Intype, London
printed in Great Britain by
Mackays of Chatham, Kent

FOR JULIUS
(born 13 August 1993)
AND
JUDITH
(again and again)

'God made me laugh,
everyone who hears of it
will laugh with me.'

Sarah to Abraham (Genesis 21.6)

'This world is not the theatre for laughter;
    neither did we come together for this intent,
that we may give way to immoderate mirth,
but that we may groan,
    and by this groaning inherit a kingdom.'

John Chrysostom[1]

'Excuse me if I cannot utter lofty words,
    but even if my eloquence meets with scorn,
my solemnity would certainly make you laugh
    had you not become unaccustomed to laughter.'

Mephistopheles to God, the Lord[2]

'Voltaire said that
heaven had given us two things
to counterbalance
the many miseries of life,
hope and sleep.
He could have added laughter.'

Immanuel Kant[3]

Contents

vii

Preface

Let's face it: there's something comic in writing 'about' laughter. Wouldn't it be better to practise laughter rather than to go on 'about' it? Don't all writers want to be taken seriously? But what is the relationship between literary seriousness and laughter? Either one writes seriously as an author, in which case readers often very soon stop laughing, or what one writes is a laugh, and then no one takes it seriously. The Tübingen philosopher Manfred Frank summed up the dilemma like this: 'If someone judges that a theory of intelligence is intelligent, that's seen as a compliment. But a theory of laughter shouldn't be laughable.'[4] And indeed anyone who sets out to read this book must be prepared for one thing: to reflect on laughter seriously enough not to lose pleasure in doing so. It is important to pursue a theory of laughter in such a way that one understands what laughter is, what functions it has, what dangers it conceals – in order perhaps to be able to laugh all the more easily.

This book is written in a situation, above all in the Catholic church, which many people would follow Karl Rahner in calling a 'wintry season'. Shivering and oppressed by the cold front of authoritarianism which prevails at present and which on many questions doesn't have the slightest sense of humour, many who are still sticking it out in the church have at best decided to hibernate.

Others have drawn the opposite conclusions. They have bidden the church farewell, with mocking laughter, because the discrepancy between their expectations and the wretchedness of reality has come to seem increasingly more grotesque. Those who nevertheless remain can hear this mocking laugh shrilling in their ears: 'You're a fool, with laughable illusions, if you still expect anything of this church. . .'

The present book seeks to provide a counterpoint to this, since neither the hiberation mentality nor mocking laugher are an appropriate expression of what must be the church's one and only concern: the person and cause of Jesus Christ. Jesus of Nazareth, crucified and risen, is the only criterion for any work in theology and the church. So this book presupposes that in Jesus' spirit of joy in both God and human beings it is possible to laugh: not because one is ignoring a reality which is often miserable and repressive, but because this laughter is the expression of an unquenchable hope, a therapy for anaesthesia of the heart: resistance to the fatalism of hibernation on the one hand and the laughter of farewell on the other. The theology of laughter attempted here is a counter-proposal to the narrow authoritarianism in the church and the rhetoric of seeing through the church, according to which all who remain are the useful idiots of the church's apparatus.

I am grateful to Dr Thomas Vogel, Cultural Editor of the Tübingen studio of Südwestfunk, for suggesting that I should deal with this topic. On his initiative a series of open lectures on 'Laughter' were given in the University of Tübingen in the winter semester of 1991/1992 in which – as is usual in such projects – representatives of a variety of disciplines participated. I was invited to play the theological part. After my lecture had appeared in a collection of papers arising out of the Tübingen series,[5] Herder Verlag asked me to develop the topic into a book. After considerable hesitation I set to work, only to discover with growing enthusiasm how many basic questions of our understanding of God and human beings are opened up by the topic of laughter, and are worth dwelling on. I hope that some spark of this enthusiasm will also come over to the reader.

So I am grateful not only to Dr Thomas Vogel and Ludger Hohn-Kemler, my editor at Herder Verlag; I am also grateful to friends and colleagues who have followed the production of the manuscript critically and have joined in by giving me many suggestions and much help: Ralf and Annette Becker of Rottweil, Gisela Bittner of Kalkar, Walter Lange of Castrop-Rauxel, and Dr Georg Langenhorst, for many years my colleague in the Institute for Ecumenical Research, to whom I owe particular thanks. Frau Ute Netuschil deserves my thanks once again for the patient, competent and efficient production of the various versions of this manuscript.

Tübingen, November 1993

Karl-Josef Kuschel

Acknowledgment

Extracts from Umberto Eco, *The Name of the Rose*, in Chapter 4 are used by the permission of the publishers, Martin Secker and Warburg and Harcourt Brace Jovanovich, Inc.

What This Book is About: A Brief Theology of Laughter

They both loved each other so much,
She was a minx and he was a thief.
When he played tricks,
She fell on the bed and laughed.

They spent the day in joy and pleasure,
At night she lay on his breast.
When they took him off to prison
She stood by the window and laughed.

He sent for her, 'O come to me,
I long for you so much,
I'm calling for you, I'm sick for you -'
She shook her head and laughed.

At six in the morning he was hanged,
at seven he was put in the grave.
And already at eight
She drank red wine and laughed.[6]

The title of this poem is 'A Woman', and no German poet but Heinrich Heine could have written such verses, with their unique mixture of frivolity and profundity. They take us right to the heart of our theme.

The woman laughs four times in this poem, but each time in a different way. There is the relaxed and joyful laughter of a woman in love, who laughs aloud at the pranks of her beloved. There is the unbelieving, apparently still superior laughter, when her beloved is suddenly taken away and as yet she has no inkling of what this means for the future. There is the ironic sarcastic laughter when the woman – apparently in contrast to her beloved – has already understood that there will be no future and it is sheer delusion still to hope for shared love. And finally there is the throwaway laughter, contemptuous of life, with which this woman follows her beloved to death...

All this already shows that writing a phenomenology of laughter is like dancing on a volcano. Hardly do you feel that you are on safe ground than it breaks away. Both laughter and life have to be kept in check, and this increases the attraction of the matter. No scientific theory and no church power has ever really been able to categorize or even control laughter. All those who have ever undertaken the task, whether as moralists or as scholastics of laughter, have exposed themselves to ridicule: nowhere, as we know, are jokes wittier than behind the backs of those who would seek to control them. So there is something laughable in any attempt to seek to create order in the realm of laughter. It's like trying to put the sea in a bottle or pack the wind in a chest. The French philosopher Henri Bergson, to whom we are indebted for a brilliant study of laughter from early in this century, was aware that laughter is not 'comprehensible', i.e. it evades any conceptual knowledge. It is like the foam on the top of a wave, and the theoretician of laughter is like a child who draws off the foam with its hand and is amazed to find that no more than a couple of drops of water run through its fingers, much more salty, much more bitter than the water of the wave which bore the foam to the sand.[7]

There is no lack of theories of laughter, of definitions of the nature and function of the comic. Philosophers, psychologists and sociologists have attempted them from Plato and Aristotle through Kant and Schopenhauer to Henri Bergson, Sigmund Freud, Helmuth Plessner and Joachim Ritter.[8] It is clear from all of them that there is no such thing as a universal theory which can explain everything comic with a single approach. Different people of different cultures and times laugh for different reasons and express very different things with their laughter. And above all, people can laugh in very different 'spirits'. There is joyful, comfortable, playful and contented laughter and there is mocking, malicious, desperate or cynical laughter. There is laughter for sheer pleasure in life and laughter from sheer bitterness at disappointments. There is affirmative, enthusiastic laughter and there is laughing at, ridiculing, on the verge of arrogance and mockery. There is proud laughter and infectious laughter, sick laughter and healing laughter. Laughter knows no limits, no tabu, no respect, and there is as much laughter at the loftiest things as at the lowliest, as much laughter at the holiest as at the most banal. Thus laughter embraces the whole spectrum of life and morality: from goodness to meanness, from humanity to barbarism. The spirit of laughter seems in principle to be the spirit of freedom, the lack of concern which reacts to distortions of reality (people pull faces to make others laugh) and is out to break down of barriers, to find an echo in a group of people.

The fact that people laugh in very different spirits makes a theology of laughter seem either humourless moralizing or a conceptual impossibility. Haven't God's representatives often enough in the past done everything possible to discredit or censure laughter? Theologies of sin and suffering are part of standard theological reflection. But a 'theology' of laughter seems inappropriate. Isn't Christian theology bound to a particular spirit, the spirit of Jesus Christ, who is at the same time the Holy Spirit of God? So mustn't a theology which is obligated to this spirit *a priori* come into conflict with the spirit of light-heartedness, heedlessness and freedom which tends to burst out in laughter? It is precisely here that the intellectual problem of a Christian theology of laughter lies: freedom and commitment, heedlessness and self-control, lack of concern and self-restraint – how do these go together? As a Christian, how does one decide, arrive at ethical criteria here without succumbing to a moralistic and humourless finger-pointing?

But haven't people always laughed in the church, *in* the church and *about* it? Aren't there plenty of jokes about popes, bishops, pastors, nuns and monks both inside and outside the church? It is impossible to overlook the fact that people have always laughed and blasphemed, especially in church, and the more repressive the current climate, the more creative the wit. This function of psychological release has long been recognized and welcomed. Particularly in church seminaries, occasions at which there is a witty take-off of the church authorities have become part of the standard repertory of church education – as a permitted means of psychological hygiene. People are ready everywhere to listen to gentle or trivial jokes, and religious bookshops, too, have their sections labelled 'Humour'.[9]

However, laughter in the church about the church is not yet a theology of laughter. Theologians who are amused at their role and what it involves need not have understood anything about the claim of such a theology. As we know, one can laugh at the church innocently or cynically. And while the one who laughs last may perhaps laugh longest, this need not be in the clearest and most far-sighted way. On the contrary, often enough 'Christian humour' proves to be superficial laughter, which is nothing but shallow opportunism, adapting to intolerable circumstances: people dispense themselves from trying to change things by a few jokes or humorous anecdotes. Those who get laughs in the evening in the bars of the more progressive church houses with their jokes about popes and bishops are often not the boldest next morning when what is needed is an open word of opposition, of civil courage within the church.

A theology of laughter must begin at a deeper level than laughable, comic phenomena in the realm of the sacred and the hierarchical, and go deeper than presenting itself in a witty, jokey, ironic and anecdotal form – as the philosopher Hans Lenk used to do not all that long ago. His *Critique of Little Reason* (1987) is subtitled 'An Introduction to Jokological Philosophy'. It is a brilliant presentation of philosophy in the form of a science of jokes in which the 'deeper significance' of philosophy is brought out with the aid of amusing paradoxes, word-plays, ideas, surprises and so on.[10]

There will be no attempt at a jokological theology here either. This book is about something different. It is not about giving laughter the occasional function of letting a breath of air into the church, but about giving it a fundamental right to a place in talk of God. A theology of laughter deserves the name only if it can understand the reality of God himself in the light of the category of laughter and define the function of such talk of God for men and women and their existence in the world. So this book begins from the basic premise that a theology of laughter derives its legitimation from the 'laughter of God' himself about the state of his creation. But what is 'the laughter of God'? In what spirit does God laugh? That is what we shall have to investigate.

As we do, it will become clear that a theology of laughter always has two sides. It reflects on the laughter of Christians and is aware of the risk of being laughed at. Like their Master from Nazareth, Christians have to take account of both laughing and being laughed at, joy and mockery, humour and malice. This duality has to be maintained – against the pessimists and the cynics, whether inside or outside the church walls. It has to be maintained by holding fast to a truth which is God himself, who, according to the basic message of scripture, is not a cynical player but a God of joy, joy in human beings and their creation. So we have to continue to trust that this God – despite all that we human beings to do his creation – does not burst into inscrutable laughter at our wretchedness but is the one of whom scripture says that he laughs with the doubters and the desperate (Abraham and Sarah) and takes more delight in the conversion of a single sinner than in ninety-nine righteous people who believe that they need no repentance.

Umberto Eco's world-famous novel *The Name of the Rose* plays an important role in this book. Indeed if one wanted to, one could call the book an answer to the challenge of this novel. Critics have called *The Name of the Rose* a typical product of the spirit of our time, the 'postmodern spirit'. That is something that we shall have to discuss. Be this as it may, in taking up the problem of laughter, this novel casts light on basic problems of philosophy and theology which I want to tackle in this book. Is there an order in the world? Is there binding truth? Can one know this order, this truth? Or does one come to grief in interpreting the 'signs' of this world, so that all that is left is resignation, the mockery of any truth? From where do we derive the basic criterion for truth? On what can we rely? By what criteria should we act if the world itself seems to be simply 'chaos' and we can recognize no order in the 'signs'?

The philosophical and theological dimensions of Eco's novel cannot, however, be understood without the European discussion of laughter, in particular not without Aristotle, for whose allegedly forgotten book about comedy all the criminal energy in Eco's book is released. And Aristotle cannot be understood without Plato's criticism of comedy and laughter, which in turn fixes on Homer. So for this book it seemed natural to begin with Homer,

Plato and Aristotle, both in view of Eco's novel and in view of the history of the Christian denunciation of laughter. I must therefore ask for the reader's patience at this point. First of all we must get at the root of the problem of laughter (which lies in Homer), before we can have the intellectual enjoyment of the play and the tension of Eco's novel.

It is also important to begin with antiquity for another reason. For a critical discussion with Eco leads to a basic question which was also discussed by the Greeks (Plato and his successors) and which we cannot avoid in this book either. Should one laugh at everything? Is laughter 'beyond good and evil'? There is no question that we live in a time in which people have grown accustomed to being able to laugh at everything. The laughter and entertainment industry is flourishing. Jokes about anything and anyone are cheap. There is no tabu which is not broken, no feeling which is not mocked, no authority which is not maliciously put in question. The present book seeks to provide a counterpoint to this. It seeks once again to raise a question which has concerned European theology from the beginning. Is laughter to be restricted? Are there limits to laughter? If so, what are they? Laughter and ethics, laughter and self-restraint, a refusal to laugh, a legitimate criticism of laughter if it is at the expense of human dignity, humanity, at the expense above all of those who are in any case weak and outcast. We cannot avoid seeking answers to these questions.

So this book is an attempt to provide a critical theology of laughter. It claims its legitimation from an indelible memory. Christians will never forget that in the bitterest hour of his life, their Master from Nazareth was one of those who were laughed at and mocked. So it will regard that kind of laughter once and for all with mistrust, hostility, indeed resistance. A critical theology of laughter will have to begin here, and each time ask in what spirit their laughter is. So an objection will be raised here to the tendentiously destructive and nihilistic character of a certain kind of laughter. It will be an objection to malicious laughter: laughter at the expense of any truthfulness, laughter which arises out of a delight in one's own wittiness and is ready to sacrifice all obligations to truthfulness on the altar of the good effect. It will be an objection to mocking laughter from above downwards:

laughter at the defenceless and marginalized, when comedy merely follows the line of the power relationships which already prevail. It will be an objection to cynical laughter: the proverbial laughter of hell, which stems from the denial of truth and ethics and which feeds on Mephistophelian anti-faith: 'So it would be better if nothing came into being.'

Indeed, if things were as they are thought to be by the Mephistopheles whom we know from the prologue in heaven to Goethe's *Faust*, we would be dealing with a God who has 'become unaccustomed to laughter': a creation which seems to have slipped from God's hand is far too sorry an affair. By contrast, this book is written in the trust that the Mephistopheleses of world history – as already in Goethe's *Faust* – do not have the last word.

I

Problems with Laughter – A Philosophical and Theological Tableau

1. Homer and the Heedless Laughter of the Gods

There is war before Troy – and the gods are banqueting on Olympus. The Greeks are besieging the city in Asia Minor under the command of their general Agamemnon – the gods are looking on from an Olympian distance and have divided their favours between the Greeks and the Trojans. While all are gathered together for the banquet on Olympus, a vigorous dispute breaks out between Zeus, the father of the gods, and his consort Hera. Zeus has just promised Thetis, goddess of the sea and the mother of the great Greek warrior Achilles, that he will support the city of Troy against the Greeks until an insult on Achilles has been avenged. Hera – who is hostile to the Trojans and supports the Greeks – has become mistrustful and jealous. Before the assembled heavenly company she provokes a violent quarrel with her spouse. Thereupon their son Hephaistos, the god of the smithy, who usually lives on the island of Lemnos, an ugly, lame, limping fellow, intervenes to calm his parents. Bustling around as cupbearer at the feast, he beseeches his mother, 'Don't press Zeus too far: he can inflict frightful punishment, just as he once took me by the ankles and threw me to earth from the threshold of heaven. I can still feel the injury.' Hera understands. Now she laughs in a friendly way, and Hephaistos, the skilful and inventive one, scurries busily round the table of the gods, dragging his leg, and pours out the wine. The mood changes:

> But among the blessed immortals uncontrollable laughter
> went up as they saw Hephaistos bustling about the palace.
> Thus thereafter the whole day long until the sun went under
> they feasted, nor was anyone's hunger denied a fair portion,
> nor denied the beautifully wrought lyre in the hands of Apollo

I

nor the antiphonal sweet sound of the Muses singing

(I, 599-604)[1]

Laughter as Schadenfreude and frivolity

There is unbounded laughter right at the beginning of European literature. Not only do human beings laugh, but so too do the gods. However, the gods laugh in a remarkably ambiguous way. We are talking about Homer, a poet who at the same time used to travel around his homeland, eighth-century Ionia in Asia Minor, singing his epic poems. The very first book of Homer's earliest epic, the *Iliad*, which was composed around 750 BCE, already reports the laughter of the gods, that 'unquenchable laughter' which has rightly become proverbial as 'Homeric laughter'. It is indeed unquenchable, this laughter of the gods, and so it is an expression of their eternal youth and power, their lack of concern and their heedlessness. These gods are capable of laughing not only at human weaknesses but also at themselves, of laughing at the weaknesses of their like.[2]

But at the same time the character of this laughter is ambiguous enough, since the gods of Olympus do not laugh out of happiness or joy; they do not laugh, say, because the tension between the supreme couple has disappeared and the banquet can now be enjoyed all the more. They do not laugh in delight and joy. They laugh from pleasure in the comic, and what they find comic we would call 'putting down'.[3] For what is comic here is the handicapped god, the god who limps as he goes bustling around the room with the drinks. He is the one who prompts the laughter and at the same time is laughed at. So the laughter of the gods is a laughter verging on malice, morally unconcerned about the weakling, who does not have the laughter on his side, but against him. The one who prompts the laughter himself becomes its object.

Thus the *Iliad* already contains an ambiguous 'miniature'[4] of the laughter of the gods, which has quite a dark side.[5] It is indeed unconcerned and heedless. How much so, is shown by another even more famous scene in which Homer once again makes us witnesses of this unique phenomenon. It can be found in the *Odyssey*, which was written around 700 BCE.[6]

Here the problem is in no way lessened by the fact that in the

2

Odyssey, in comparison to the *Iliad*, the world of the gods seems to have a more marked ethical dimension in which the laughter of the gods is to some degree alluded to in quotation marks, and is really already a 'foreign body'.[7] Certainly it is true that the scene with the laughter of the gods in the *Odyssey* is not reported by the narrator himself, as it is in the *Iliad*, but is a song within a song. In the eighth book of the *Odyssey* the singer Demodokos in fact presents this laughter episode as a dance song to relax the tensions in festivities which have gone sour, and it promptly has the desired effect. But this story of the laughter of the gods, too, is presented without any criticism of the gods, whose behaviour in the *Odyssey* remains as ambiguous as it is in the *Iliad*. Though here too a quotation from the world of the *Iliad* may have been used, it is hardly an alien body. For the quotation does not lead to detachment from the laughter of the gods but to identification with it. What are we talking about?

Once again we have laughter associated with Hephaistos. The starting point in the *Odyssey* is already incomparably more comic than that in the *Iliad*. For Hephaistos has married Aphrodite, the goddess of beauty and love. The comic side of this combination is manifest to any reader: Hephaistos, who is certainly inventive, but unattractive because he is always so grimy – and Aphrodite, who is quite lovely, attractive, radiant with beauty. Can the relationship last? No. For Aphrodite has no intention of remaining faithful to her ugly, handicapped and crude spouse. Instead, she has an affair with Ares, the radiant god of war. However, she has the misfortune to have her adultery discovered by the sun god Helios, from whom nothing remains hidden anyway, and this is disclosed to Hephaistos.

Raging with jealousy, Hephaistos forges a plan of revenge. He pretends to go on a journey, but previously has skilfully constructed an invisible net over the lovers' bed, and in it the two of them are promptly trapped. Informed by Helios of the success of his trap, Hephaistos rushes home. Pointing to the adulterers wriggling in the bed, he rages furiously against heaven and calls on the gods to become witnesses of his shame:

Father Zeus and all you other blessed immortal
gods, come here, to see a ridiculous sight, no seemly

matter, how Aphrodite daughter of Zeus forever
holds me in little favour, but she loves ruinous Ares
because he is handsome, and goes sound on his feet, while I
    am
misshapen from birth, and for this I hold no other responsible
but my own father and mother, and I wish they never had got
    me.
Now look and see, where these two have gone to bed and lie
    there
in love together. I am sickened when I look at them, and yet
I think they will not go on lying thus even for a little,
much though they are in love, I think they will have no wish
for sleeping, but my fastenings and my snare will contain them
until her father pays back in full all my gifts of courtship
I paid out into his hand for the sake of his bitch-eyed daughter.
The girl is beautiful indeed, but she is intemperate

(VIII, 306-320).

We must call to mind all the aspects of this scene. For here we have more than the tale of the buffoonery of a cuckolded husband; here is plainly the story of a cheated man, a man who is ugly and who is now having an ugly game played on him, a man who was already physically afflicted and is now being inwardly hurt. Moreover Hephaistos's lament is literally heart-breaking. The 'laughter of things' is apparent for him, but only apparently. In reality the situation is unbearable for one who came into the world a cripple and now must look on while the last remnant of his self-respect is similarly crippled. No wonder that this tormented figure does not complain only about this particular shameful moment. What is shattering is that Hephaistos evidently sees the need on this occasion literally to put the ground of his existence in question. This cripple has evidently understood that it is the gods themselves, indeed the supreme gods, Zeus and Hera, who have brought him into this world. And these are the very gods who now bestow this fate on him: to be the limping one who is eternally mocked and is now also deceived. No wonder that Hephaistos puts the 'blame' for his fate not merely superficially on Ares and Aphrodite, but really on those who gave birth to him, the supreme divine couple. They are the real culprits, and therefore he accuses them. The bitterest reproach that children can make

4

to their parents is put on the lips of Hephaistos: 'I wish you had never got me!'

But how do the gods react? It is striking that neither Zeus nor Hera react to their son's cry for help. In any case the goddesses stay at home, 'for shame', as we are explicitly told; such a scene of adultery is evidently not for women – even by the standards of Olympus. Only a few male gods come: Poseidon, Hermes and Apollo. But how do they react when they see the adulterers caught in the net? Are they full of 'shame', full of moral indignation? Are they ready to give a demonstration here of dignity and respect? Will they at least show solidarity with the victim? Not at all.

And among the blessed immortals uncontrollable laughter
went up as they saw the handiwork of subtle Hephaistos
(VIII, 326-7).

That is one thing: the three gods first of all laugh out of sheer *Schadenfreude* at the deceived deceivers, and are vastly amused at the trap which Hephaistos has constructed and successfully laid.

But there is more: certainly the three gods use moral vocabulary in the very next sentence: 'No virtue in bad dealings. See, the slow one has overtaken the swift.' But it immediately becomes clear that this moralizing is only pseudo-moralizing, irony. For at the same time one of the gods, Apollo, cannot help making a frivolous comment on this scene. Apollo says to Hermes:

Hermes, son of Zeus, guide and giver of good things, tell me,
would you caught tight in these strong fastenings, be willing
to sleep in bed by the side of Aphrodite the golden?
(VIII, 335-7)

And Hermes replies,

Lord who strikes from afar, Apollo, I wish it could only
be, and there could be thrice this number of endless fastenings,
and all you gods could be looking on and all the goddesses,
and still would I sleep by the side of Aphrodite the golden
(339-42).

In other words, for all their apparent moral indignation ('Evil never flourishes'), the male gods have no thought of restraining their male fantasies. Hermes says what Apollo is also thinking:

5

taking everything into account, even the fetters, the trap and the voyeurism of gods and goddesses (!), it would be worthwhile sleeping just once with 'golden Aphrodite'. And promptly we also hear a second time:

He spoke, and there was laughter among the immortals.

This time it is not malicious laughter, not the laughter of *Schaden-freude*, but a laughter of frivolity, of suggestive fantasy. Already on Olympus the atmosphere seems to have been rather like that of today in many male locker rooms...

Laughter without ethics: Homer's ambiguity

Such scenes, which mock ideas, institutions and customs comically and crudely with the aid of ironic distortion or farcical caricature, are called 'divine burlesques'. They are not unusual in Greek literature. At the time of the *Iliad* and the *Odyssey* they were still part of the religious world of the Greeks, without being made tabu or criticized. Presumably older than Homeric epic, the divine carnival is part of an age-old stratum of myth which is evidently not felt to conflict with the task of the gods. On the contrary, such laughter is evidently compatible with the 'dignity of the gods'. It was not felt offensive, though – as the philologist Robert Muth rightly writes – it is 'far removed from all calculating human reason'.[8]

That is in fact the decisive thing here: the gods are evidently far above not only all human reason but also all calculating ethics. And precisely this – for all the amusement here – makes the phenomenon of the thoughtless 'Homeric laughter of the gods' something which is far from being harmless. For in fact these gods are not to be measured by moral categories, although it is the gods who should be guarantors of the moral law. Their laughter is an expression of their lack of concern for ethical criteria, of which they themselves are the guarantors. Whereas the beginnings of a divine world with a more thought-out ethic may may already be present in the *Odyssey*, when it comes to the laughter of the gods, at any rate, the two epics are clearly no different. In both texts the laughter of the gods knows no compassion for the weak, no mercy for the afflicted, no sparing of the innocent, no solidarity with the victims.

So the unsuspecting reader of Homer should not be deceived: the gods described here do not become, say, 'more human', 'more pleasant' as a result of their laughter. For all the anthropomorphism of the phenomenon of laughter they are not, say, like human beings and thus subject to human categories. On the contrary, in none of the gods does the laughter lose its power and force, its 'tremendous superiority, freedom and certainty'![9] The gods remain incalculable: in an ultimately uncanny way incomprehensible. So we do not do justice to the Homeric gods if we want, say, to set off their laughter off against the 'inscrutable laughter of the Indian god'. For the laughter at Hephaistos, the comic cripple, is anything but 'shallow laughter'.[10] On the contrary, the Greek scholar Paul Friedländer is right in saying: 'The metaphysics of this Olympian laughter first dawns when we hear it ringing out above the ten thousand griefs of the Achaeans.'[11] He is referring to the griefs of the Greeks, thousands of whom are involved in a bloody life-and-death battle with the Trojans, while the gods look down on the battle and at a cheerful Olympian distance distribute their sympathies and antipathies between the different sides. The Homeric laughter from the distant, cheerful world of the gods rings out over the battlefield with its piles of corpses.

No wonder that such stories about the gods became less and less convincing in Greece, the more that philosophical and ethical reason began to come into their own. Criticism gradually extended to these frivolous and thus morally ambiguous traits of the Homeric gods. While it may already be partially recognizable in the *Odyssey*, it can first clearly be seen in a contemporary of Homer's, the epic poet Hesiod from Askra in Boeotia. We know that Hesiod regarded Homer's world of the gods as a world of deceptive appearances. So in his works the gods are no longer the cheerful Olympians but powerful, lofty, even beneficial powers upon whose rule human beings look with reverent fear. Hesiod's picture of Zeus is no longer that of a father god torn in different directions by the passions and ultimately incalculable, but that of a real guarantor of law, justice, and order, who has granted human beings an existence which, while it is certainly laborious, is nevertheless just.

Moreover, in his second *magnum opus* after the *Theogony*, the *Works and Days*, Hesiod significantly makes clear the difference

7

from Homer's world by the laughter of Zeus. First of all Hesiod explains with the help of the Prometheus myth why the gods kept food 'hidden' from human beings, and therefore why human beings have to work so laboriously for their sustenance. Hesiod's answer is that this is because Prometheus (son of Iapetos) attempted to deceive Zeus by stealing fire from him:

> And so he thought of painful cares for men.
> First he hid fire, but the son of Iapetos
> Stole it from Zeus the Wise, concealed the flame
> In a fennel stalk, and fooled the Thunderer.
> Then, raging, spoke the Gatherer of clouds:
> 'Prometheus, most crafty god of all,
> You stole the fire and tricked me, happily,
> You, plague on all mankind and on yourself.
> They'll pay for fire: I'll give another gift
> To men, an evil thing for their delight,
> And all will love this ruin in their hearts.'

This explains the human situation: the deception of Zeus by Prometheus. As a punishment the god sends evil to human beings, but immediately after this passage there is a description of the creation of the fair Pandora, whose 'box of evils' is opened when Epimetheus, the brother of Prometheus, cannot help embracing her. And since, according to Hesiod, Zeus foresees all this evil that befalls human beings, he laughs – the superior laughter of a god who will not allow anyone to play tricks on him. The very next sentence says:

> So spoke the father of men and gods, and laughed.[12]

Zeus laughs as the one who tells human beings of their ill-fortune. In Hesiod we no longer hear anything of the laughter of the gods at their like, as in Homer; in the laughter of Zeus we perceive only the superiority of the creator of the worlds and human beings, who calls into being as it pleases him and punishes cheating tricks like those of Prometheus with ills that affect all men and women. The parallels to the creation story in the Hebrew Bible are unmistakable. Certainly Yahweh is not known for laughing at the fall of humankind, but in their power as creator and their function as guarantor of law and order the two 'gods' have comparable features.

8

Criticism of the Homeric gods intensified further in the following centuries. For the more that philosophy and ethics became established, the more the anthropomorphic image of the gods that had been shaped by Homer was subjected to radical criticism. Heraclitus, the philosopher from Ephesus (towards the end of the sixth century), was already calling for Homer to be banished from the cultic festivals into which in the meantime the performance of rhapsodies had made its way; indeed Homer was to be chastized with the rod.[13] In his plays, Aristophanes (c.445-c.385) the comic poet mocked the Homeric gods as fabrications of human fantasy.[14] And finally there was Plato, the Athenian philosopher who pointed out the moral danger of poetry, especially that of Homer, above all in his teaching about the state. It is worth going into this more closely. What lies behind such criticism, the attempt of the philosophers to dominate laughter and bring it under political and moral control? At the beginning of European philosophy there was no uncontrollable and heedless laughter, as in literature; at the beginning of European philosophy an attempt was made to tame laughter.

2. Plato and Indignation at Laughter

In Homer the gods laugh, unconcerned and heedless; in Plato the philosophers, i.e. those who truly know, are reluctant to laugh. Why? Because for Plato what human beings laugh at and what prompts this laughter in a person is something fundamentally inferior, reprehensible. This answer at any rate can be read in one of the late dialogues of Plato (427-347), the *Philebos*, which 'is perhaps the first, and at any rate the oldest, extant theory of laughter and the laughable'.[15]

The ethical taming of laughter

In his dialogue Plato begins from two basic questions. First, who and what are to be laughed at? For Plato, above all people who fail to know themselves, i.e. who succumb to deception about themselves, whether in the material, physical or spiritual sphere. It is laughable, ridiculous, when someone regards himself as richer, greater or morally better than he really is, because when one gets to know his tricks one can see through him.

9

Secondly, what sparks off laughter? What effects does it have in an encounter? According to Plato, anyone who is confronted with people in whom there is a discrepancy between appearance and essence, imagination and reality, and laughs, feels in the affective realm a remarkable mixture of distaste and pleasure. Plato's word for this is *phtomos*, which is best translated – following Hans Georg Gadamer – as a basic mood of 'rivalry anxiety'.[16] In other words, the possible superiority of another person on the one hand prompts anxiety (distaste), and on the other hand relief (pleasure), since the other is not really superior but only apparently so. This mixture is then expressed in the boundless laughter of *Schadenfreude*, a 'comic pleasure' which has something quite aggressive about it, so that Plato was already given the credit of 'having discovered the aggressive element in laughter',[17] which was correctly analysed as such only by the behavioural scientists of the twentieth century.

Be this as it may, what is decisive for understanding Plato's theory of laughter is that Plato first discusses laughter from an interpersonal aspect and secondly sees 'comic pleasure' as something inferior. Already in Plato there is an association of a theory of laughter and ethical judgment which is to prove momentous for European intellectual history. Thus Plato develops the first basic theme of the future theory of laughter: laughter and ethics belong together. The unbridled, boundless dynamic of laughter must be ethically tamed. So for the first time in Plato laughter is subjected to a moral judgment: 'Plato censures "comic pleasure" to the degree that it arises from an unjust attitude at the expense of fellow human beings, who are not commiserated with in their wretched state, although they are not enemies.'[18]

So why is the philosopher reluctant to laugh in Plato? We can now give a twofold answer on the basis of Plato's other writings.

1. The philosopher discovers the laughable element in other human beings (Plato's dialogues are full of this), but it is his fundamental task to enlighten those around him who are not philosophical about their self-deceptions, and any rate make them aware of the true being beyond all appearance.

2. The philosopher avoids laughter as a reaction to the laughable because it arises from a 'comical pleasure', an ethically question-able *Schadenfreude*. In this way the philosopher loses precisely

what is meant to mark him out: moderation in all things, the mean between the extremes, and thus his identity and integrity. So in other writings, too, Plato condemned above all unbridled laughter and argued that excess should be avoided in both joy and pain and that dignity should be preserved by the observation of the right mean.[19]

The philosopher – laughed at and laughing

But there is something else that we must see in Plato. In fulfilling his task, the philosopher can himself be one of those who are laughed at, just as he can occasionally also unmask the pseudo-world of human beings by an act of laughter. The brief anecdote about the natural philosopher Thales of Miletus which Plato makes his Socrates tell in the dialogue *Theaetetus* is famous:

> I will illustrate my meaning by the jest which the clever witty Thracian handmaid is said to have made about Thales, when he fell into a well as he was looking up at the stars. She said that he was so eager to know what was going on in heaven that he could not see what was before his feet.[20]

This anecdote shows the philosopher as a comic figure, and since then the 'laughter of the Thracian woman' has rung down through the history of philosophy: Hans Blumenberg has investigated its waves in loving detail down to Nietzsche.[21] That is a worthwhile investigation, since this laughter is an almost archetypal expression of the resistance of the nearest to the farthest, of everyday life to pure theory, of sound human understanding to philosophical eccentricity.

Plato was also aware of this, and so the dialectical effect of his story was important. For the one who has true knowledge, the philosopher, must necessarily seem laughable to the unphilosophical person. Why? Because he sees 'more' than what is nearest and everyday, because he attempts to see through the surface of life to the 'essence' of things. That is why the laughter of the Thracian woman and all those who down the centuries have laughed at the philosophers for their 'other-worldliness' rebounds on the one who laughs, because in her laughter she merely shows her own limitations, how she is imprisoned in what is nearest to hand. But the philosopher – as we can also read in the *Theaetetus* – can also laugh – in a superior way at those who remain imprisoned in the superficial and the inflated (panegyrics to kings or important families); he is the one who can distinguish between *doxa* and *aletheia*, between appearance and being, ignorance and truth, education and wisdom.[22]

So we are fully justified in speaking of a second fundamental theme in Plato's theory of laughter: insight into the dialectic of laughing and being laughed at, whenever someone is concerned with the truth. According to Plato, anyone who knows the truth also knows this experience: one is laughed at by all those who regard this truth as scandalous, idiotic or illusory, and at the same time the one who knows laughs at the ignorance, superficiality and naivety of those who laugh at him. We shall encounter this dialectic again in the sphere of Christianity.

Why 'Homeric laughter' is harmful

That helps us to understand better why for Plato the art-form of laughter, comedy, must be inferior to philosophy because of its markedly affective character. It in particular belongs in the sphere of whatever is not serious, of appearances. So it is not surprising that Plato also goes into the problem of laughter in connection with his theory of poetry. We understand the problem that laughter raises here only if we are clear about the 'nature of poetry' as Plato sees it.

For Plato, two aspects of poetry must be distinguished: the ontological and the moral-paedogogical. First of all the ontological aspect. In the tenth book of his *Republic*, a dialogue between Socrates and the brothers Adeimantos and Glaukon, Plato unmistakably explains to us what degree of reality and thus what status of truth poetry has for him. The lowest of all! As is well known, according to Plato the highest level of truth is that of the eternal, imperishable, perfect 'ideas', beyond the transitory, imperfect world of appearances. This world of 'ideas' is the world of true being. Everything that exists on earth is already a secondary and worse reality, broken appearance, an imperfect copy of the perfect ideas.

An example which Plato himself chooses is a shoe. A craftsman, a shoemaker, does not invent the 'idea' of the shoe but finds it already there and makes the shoe in accordance with this eternal 'idea'; in keeping with his profession, this shoe is imperfect, since everything is imperfect and apparent in comparison with the perfect idea and the true being. But there are also craftsmen who do not make particular things but merely imitate (*mimesis*), i.e. just copy what is already there. These craftsmen include the painters. And their pictures? What are these if not imitations of particular things already made by other craftsmen? So the shoe made by the shoemaker has a similar relationship to the shoe painted by the painter to that between the 'idea' of the shoe and the shoemaker's shoe. The degree of perfection, the content of the essence, diminishes here from one stage to the next. The painter is not imitating the 'idea' (as is the shoemaker in the case of the shoe), but merely copying a reality which has already been made by the craftsman. Moreover the painter need not understand anything about the craft of making the shoe which he paints. He is not 'really' making a shoe but merely imitating one. In other words, the painter is essentially making nothing but illusory depictions of copies. From the original image (the 'idea', the essence) to the copy (the object made) to the illusory depiction (art) there is a triple loss of reality and thus truth. If the products of the shoemaker are already imperfect and mere appearance compared with the ideas, the products of the artists are even more so.

What is true of painting is also true of poetry. Since it too is nothing but imitation in the sense of a description of human beings, events and actions, it too falls under Plato's 'ontological declaration of nothingness'.[23] For from an ontological perspective poetry has as little worth as painting. That is true of poetry from Homer to the poets of the day. Moreover Plato makes his Socrates say unmistakably in the *Republic*:

> Then must we not infer that all these poetical individuals, beginning with Homer, are only imitators; they copy images of virtue and the like, but the truth they never reach? The poet is like a painter who, as we have already observed, will make a likeness of a cobbler though he understand nothing of cobbling; and his picture is good enough for those who know no more than he does, and judge only by colours and figures... In like manner the poet with his words and phrases may be said to lay on the colours of the several arts, himself understanding their

nature only enough to imitate them, and other people, who are as ignorant as he is, and judge only from his words, imagine that if he speaks of cobbling, or of military tactics, or of anything else, in metre and harmony and rhythm, he speaks very well – such is the sweet influence which melody and rhythm by nature have.[24]

What follows from this for Plato? 'The imitator has no knowledge worth mentioning of what he imitates. Imitiation is only a kind of play or sport.'[25]

Poetry – a game, nothing serious; an illusion, not reality; a lie, not the truth. The pedagogical-moral condemnation corresponds to the ontological one. It is described at length in the second and third books of the *Republic*, at the centre of which is the question of the nature of justice. This question is elevated by the partners in the dialogue beyond the individual and interpersonal level and discussed in concrete terms, politically and socially, in connection with the model of an ideal state. One of the questions is: in this state, who belongs to the classes which support it? Answer: the *demiurgoi*, the workers (e.g. farmers and craftsman), then the 'guardians' (*phylakes*) and then the 'rulers' (*archontes*). So Plato has the idea of a state with three classes which have a strict hierarchical division from below upwards.

The partners in the conversation do not analyse the lowest class, that of the workers, in further detail. We are presented with a wealth of important professions which are indispensable to the state, without any concern to give any of them an individual profile. Things already change when we get to the next class up, that of the guardians. They already have a good deal of responsibility for the wellbeing of the whole state. So the question of their correct education (*paideia*) must also be discussed. For according to Plato, in addition to characteristics like bravery and watchfulness, the guardians must also have a philosophical nature. And that includes musical education, gymnastic training of the body and schooling in music and literature. The question automatically arises: what literature is most suitable for this class of guardians? What can best contribute to furthering the 'chief virtue' of the guardians, i.e. bravery?

Homer? Can Homer with all his frivolous stories of the gods, all his episodes of passion, anger, joy, sensuality, even among the gods, be a candidate for this? Plato has serious doubts. However popular Homer may still have been in his time, this literature seems inappropriate for a state of the future. It should not be read. One example Plato gives is laughter. Are the stories of the feelings of the gods which Homer reports, the passion and the laughter, appropriate for bringing up the young? If even gods display extreme expressions of feeling, how are the 'guardians' to be brought up to be brave and fear God? How are they to find the 'right mean' between the extremes which is so important for Plato, the ideal of the most cheerful repose and self-control? Here is Socrates to Adeimantos:

For if, my sweet Adeimantos, our youth seriously listen to such unworthy representations of the gods, instead of laughing at them as they ought, hardly will any of them deem that he himself, being but a man, can be dishonoured by similar actions; neither will he rebuke any inclination which may arise in his mind to say and do the like. And instead of having any shame or self-control, he will be always whining and lamenting on slight occasions.

Yes, he said, that is most true...

Yes, I replied, but that surely is what ought not to be, as the argument has just proved to us; and by that proof we must abide until it is disproved by a better.

It ought not to be.

Neither ought our guardians to be given to laughter. For a fit of laughter which has been indulged to excess almost always produces a violent reaction.

So I believe.

Then persons of worth, even if only mortal men, must not be represented as overcome by laughter, and still less must such a representation of the gods be allowed.

Still less of the gods, as you say, he replied.

Then we shall not suffer such an expression to be used about the gods as that of Homer when he describes how

'Uncontrollable laughter arose among the blessed gods, when they saw Hephaistos bustling about the mansion.'

On your views, we must not admit them.[26]

So what is the true task of poetry? Not to depict such a perverse world which only leads youth astray in their quest for the right mean. The task of poetry is the portrayal of virtues and of great moral actions. Its task is above all the composition of hymns of praise to the gods and the rulers. True poetry only has the task of improving people, and only such poetry will be allowed in the future state! Wisdom is the cardinal virtue of the rulers, bravery that of the guardians, observing a sensible mean that of the workers, and perfect justice prevails as the fourth Platonic cardinal virtue when each member of a class does 'his own thing', i.e. fulfils in the most perfect way the virtue which befits him.

And what about the old poetry à la Homer? It has no place in this theory of state virtue and education. For it addresses only the lower powers of the soul, the drives. Such poetry describes human beings and even gods who act irrationally, full of passions, and this leads the reader to complain and lament about such examples and even find satisfaction in so doing. Such poetry only nurtures uncontrollable feelings and in this way destroys reason. Such poets lie in telling false stories about the gods. But what about the divine? Is it not 'completely free from error and deception'? In that case how can poets say of gods that they are 'conjurers' who change into different forms? How can such poetry 'deceive by lie in word and work'?[27] Away with such products – they need to be banned from a future ideal state!

3. Aristotle and the Permissible Function of Laughter

Laughter as the expression of unrestrained drives, as a loss of moderation: Plato's critical theory of laughter (not to be confused with a repudiation of jests, humour and cheerfulness) did not go uncontradicted, though none of his pupils dared to criticize him directly. But Aristotle (384-322) did not think of following his teacher in such a fundamental moral condemnation of particular poems and indignation about laughter. Certainly, even Aristotle would not justify and allow laughter in its extremes: here he remained the pupil of Plato, whose Academy he had entered in 367 at the age of seventeen and in which he was to spend twenty years until Plato's death. But Aristotle evidently did not see why one should not allow laughter for particular useful functions, as a way of taming it.

Anyway, Aristotle was more prepared than Plato to attach a significance for philosophy to what was this-worldly and real, to what could be observed and experienced in concrete terms. He did not want *a priori* to link all philosophy to 'transcendence', but unconditionally to begin from reality as given. So scientific studies (through physics, biology and meteorology to a natural history and morphology of animals and a psychology of the human 'soul') play a decisive role in Aristotle. He was interested in collecting and interpreting a wealth of natural material in order to penetrate through the empirical facts to universal principles.

This also had consequences for his assessment of laughter. In one of his works of natural philosophy, *Parts of Animals*, Aristotle had also inserted a fundamental comment on laughter; for the ancients the diaphragm was regarded as the 'seat' of laughter: 'That when heated the diaphragm quickly makes the sensation recognizable is afforded by what happens when we laugh. When people are tickled, they quickly burst into laughter, and this is because the motion quickly penetrates to this part, and even though it is only gently warmed, still it produces a movement (independently of the will) in the intelligence which is recognizable. The fact that human beings only are susceptible to tickling is due 1. to the fineness of their skin and 2. to their being the only creatures who laugh.'[28]

So Aristotle's intention was not to devalue laughter *a priori* in a moralizing way. As a natural scientist he was first of all interested in a concrete physiological and biological definition of laughter. On purely empirical grounds it was already an incontrovertible fact for him that human beings differ from all other living beings by virtue of their capacity to laugh. The *proprium hominis*, the distinctive characteristic of human beings which distinguishes them from all animals, lies in their capacity to laugh. Whatever can laugh is human. And what is human can laugh. Friedrich Nietzsche was later to give pointed expression to this insight: 'The sorriest animal on earth invented laughter.'[29] No wonder that in other of his works, too, Aristotle sought to understand laughter, or better sought how to deal properly with this phenomenon which is so evidently human, indeed is distinctive of human beings. He analyses laughter within the framework of ethics, rhetoric and poetics.

The irony of the refined: the ideal of the mean

First of all there is Aristotle's ethical *magnum opus*, the *Nicomachean Ethics*, dedicated to his son Nicomachos, which pursues two main thoughts: first, the definition of the goal (or better the activity) of the good, which Aristotle calls *eudaimonia*, 'happiness'; and secondly the capacity which makes this activity possible, governing one's own conduct by reason. But when, for Aristotle, is a person's own action or conduct determined by reason? When – in a particular individual instance – the mean (*mesotes*) has been found between two possible extremes. Only the criterion of the mean is appropriate for human beings.

This quest for the ideal mean also applies to the phenomenon of laughter. So in his ethics Aristotle compares the free man to the buffoon, the person who has not found this mean: 'Those who carry humour to excess are thought to be vulgar buffoons, striving after humour at all cost, and aiming rather at raising a laugh than at saying what is becoming and at avoiding pain to the object of their fun; while those who can neither make a joke themselves nor put up with those who do are thought to be boorish and unpolished. But those who joke in a tasteful way are called ready-witted, which implies a sort of readiness to turn this way and that.'[30]

But who jests in an 'appropriate' way? For Aristotle, between the extreme types (the humourless person and the buffoon) is the ironist, who found his ideal model in Socrates: 'Ironic people, who understate things, seem more attractive in character; for they are thought to speak not for gain but to avoid parade; and here too it is qualities which bring reputation that they disclaim, as Socrates used to do. Those who disclaim trifling and obvious qualities are called humbugs and are more contemptible; and sometimes this seems to be boastfulness, like the Spartan dress; for both excess and great deficiencies are boastful. But those who use understatement with moderation and understate about matters that do not very much force themselves on our notice seem attractive.'[31] So that was Aristotle's concern in matters of laughter: to find the right mean between a lack of humour and buffoonery.

There is a second point: already in the *Nicomachean Ethics* a social, class-specific element can be recognized. Aristotle already sees that the aristocrats and the educated should jest differently from the common crowd: 'The well-bred man's jesting differs from that of a vulgar man, and the joking of an educated man from that of an uneducated... The refined and well-bred man therefore will be as we have described, being as it were a law to himself. Such, then, is the man who observes the mean, whether he be called tactful or ready-witted. The buffoon, on the other hand, is the slave of his sense of humour, and spares neither himself nor others if he can raise a laugh, and says things none of which a man of refinement would say, and to some of which he would not even listen. The boor again is useless for such social intercourse, for he contributes nothing and finds fault with everything. But relaxation and amusement are thought to be a necessary element in life.'[32]

That the educated and aristocrats should talk differently from the uneducated crowd was something that the court tutor Aristotle (whose most important pupil was Alexander of Macedon, later called 'the Great') took for granted. No wonder that reflections to this effect can also be found in his theory of public speaking, his *Rhetoric*. Here too, without any moralizing undertone and pedagogical aim, Aristotle coolly and soberly analyses the function of speech, for whatever purpose one may use it. What function can laughter have here?

The usefulness of laughter: Rhetoric *and* Poetics

Laughter has a useful function for the orator, for example at the bar of the court! 'Confound the opponents' earnest with jest and their jest with earnest,'[33] declares Aristotle, and at this point for everything else refers to his *Poetics*, where there is an account of how many kinds of laughable things there are, some of which are open to a free person to mention and others are not: 'You should therefore choose the kind that suits you. Irony is more gentlemanly than buffoonery if the first is employed on one's own account, the second on that of another.'[34]

So let's keep to the *Poetics*, a book which historically speaking represents the first attempt to investigate literature exclusively in terms of its construction, its 'design'. Here, too, the contrast with Plato is unmistakable. Poetry is understood as *mimesis*, as an imitation of reality, and not primarily in terms of its pedagogical, moral or political aim. Moreover Aristotle was not prepared simply to take over the threefold gradation of reality which Plato had asserted. He subjected the Platonic ontology, the theory of ideas, to a radical reinterpretation. For Aristotle there are no ideas independently of things; for him that would amount to an absurd duplication of reality. Rather, the ideas (Aristotle speaks of 'form') indwell the things of the world of appearances. There is no 'idea' of things beyond the many individual things, rather, the 'idea' (or the 'form') of things is realized only through the individual things. Nor does any 'idea' (or 'form') of things exist without the many individual things.

This also had consequences for his assessment of works of art, of poetry. For according to Aristotle the work of art does not depict mere copies, but reality. For him, in contrast to Plato, a work of art is no longer the imitation of a second stage, but an imitation of the first and only stage, and this also gives the artist another status: the position occupied by the craftsman in Plato. That made it clear that the new theory of being 'took the ground from under the ontologically grounded declassing of poetry undertaken by Plato in the tenth book of the *Republic*'.[35] Now poetry need not be seen *a priori* in its moral ambiguity, but can be analysed soberly and in a matter-of-fact way in terms of its functions in respect of affects, passions and emotions, just as the physician soberly and objectively analyses dangerous matter with a view to using it ultimately to improve health.

Moreover, just how functionally and rationally Aristotle regards laughter and comedy emerges from the *Poetics*. The beginning of this book promises deep insights into the phenomenon of laughter. For right at the beginning of the *Poetics* tragedy and comedy are treated with the same weight. According to Aristotle, in both cases the poetic art has emerged from two natural causes: the urge to imitate which is innate to human beings from childhood, and the delight in imitating things which other people have made. Both tragedy and comedy have these roots. And a man like Homer mastered forms which led to both: the epics *Iliad* and *Odyssey* to tragedy and the Homeric satire *Margites* to comedy.

But what is the difference between tragedy and comedy? In the depiction of characters, 'Comedy would make its personages worse, and tragedy better, than the men of the present day.' In other words, while comedy depicts unusually bad people, it is concerned only with that badness which falls within the sphere of the laughable. To quote Aristotle: 'As for comedy, it is an imitation of men worse than the average; worse, however, not as regards every sort of fault, but only as regards one particular kind, the ridiculous, which is a species of the ugly.'[36] For Aristotle, while the laughable is a mistake, a defect, it does not have painful or damaging consequences. Now follows a first fundamental definition of the laughable, the ridiculous: 'The ridiculous may be defined as a mistake or deformity not productive of pain or harm to others. The mask, for instance, that excites laughter is something ugly and distorted without causing pain.'[37] This fundamental definition leaves much to be desired, especially when Aristotle promises at an early stage: 'Reserving comedy for consideration later, let us now proceed to the discussion of tragedy'.[38]

And indeed, only the problems of tragedy are discussed in the first book of Aristotle's *Poetics*. In the second book Aristotle turned to comedy and thus to the theory of the ridiculous and the comic. The only problem is that while Aristotle indeed wrote this second book of his *Poetics* – according to testimony from antiquity – it has not come down to us. Only the first half of the *Poetics* has lasted through time. The second half with the discussion of comedy has been lost, so for comedy we must essentially be content with the sparse allusions which Aristotle made in the writings already mentioned.

It becomes clear that in contrast to Plato, Aristotle does not condemn laughter in principle but attempts as it were to tame it by regarding it as having certain limited useful and therefore legitimate functions:

- Laughter is a characteristic of human beings, and indeed distinguishes them from animals.
- In principle laughter is not morally reprehensible, but can serve to refresh, to attract, to relax.

- Laughter is not inferior, but a legitimate way, for example, of combatting opponents in court. But not every form of the ridiculous is appropriate for the 'free man'. He must strive for the ideal mean between no sense of humour and buffoonery.
- Laughter has its own art form, comedy, and can be tamed in that.
- What is ridiculous in a comedy is what is ugly by virtue of some defect, without this causing pain or corruption.

Thus far the facts. But what if...?

4. Aristotle, Umberto Eco and *The Name of the Rose*

But what if in northern Italy on the slopes of the Apennines at the beginning of the fourteenth century there had been a Benedictine monastery, famous throughout Christianity for its unique library, whose giant tower dominated the whole monastery complex? What if in this same Benedictine monastery there had been wise monks, versed in the art of copying, illustrating and restoring books, who had managed to come upon the traces of a mystery which had been cunningly and shrewdly guarded up until then by the Spaniard Jorge de Burgos, the head of the library, who had become very old and blind? A man who despite his blindness was the only one who knew the mysterious, labyrinthine depths of this library tower, he and some of his helpers...?

A monastery, a library and a secret

Let us imagine that around the end of the year 1327 an English Franciscan monk comes to this monastery. He is on his way to fulfil a tricky political mission – the background is the great political game between the German emperor (Ludwig of Bavaria) and the Pope (John XXII in Avignon). On the surface he is to defend his order before the tribunal of the papal Inquisition, which is to meet in this monastery. The point of dispute is how the ideal of Christ's poverty is to be lived out in the papal church. But at a deeper level William is a pawn in the game of the German emperor, who wants to use the conflict over poverty in the church to weaken papal authority.

Hardly has the visitor, William of the Baskerville family, arrived, than he is confronted with an unprecedented series of deaths. One monk has jumped from a window, for reasons which have not yet been explained; another is found the next day in a butt containing pigs' blood; a third is found the day after in the bath house. Commissioned by the abbot of the monastery to clear up these mysterious deaths before the inquisitors arrive, William himself now penetrates deeper and deeper into the labyrinthine abysses of this monastery. Does the brilliant plan of a criminal mastermind lies behind all these deaths? Or is an apocalyptic judgment being inflicted in this chain of mysterious events: every day a crime with a specific 'sign' (hail, blood, water etc.), which seems to be suggested by the secret Revelation of John? Is the order presented by the story within the framework (seven days, each day ordered by the monastic hours of prayer) a real order? Or is everything ruled by blind chance, by chaos and whim?

That is the starting point of a book which appeared in 1980 and became a world-wide bestseller for its exciting story, the refined subtlety of its references and its witty allusions to historical figures, along with works on the history of philosophy, theology and literature. The book was *The Name of the Rose*, written by Umberto Eco, who was born in 1932 in Alessandria in Piedmont, and had previously made a name for himself as a university professor of 'semiotics', the art and theory of 'sign systems'.[39]

The multiplicity of the references, the many layers of the signs in this novel, already becomes clear from its narrative technique. The narrative is deliberately interconnected: with visible satisfaction in his literary ploy and fictitious masquerades the author hides himself in many ways, deliberately and constantly confusing the reader with ever new adventurous disguises. This method is immediately evident from the fact that the novel really has three beginnings. With the first of these, under the title, 'Naturally a manuscript', the author seems ironically to be caricaturing his own enterprise. Eco goes on in the same opening chapter by creating a fourfold manuscript fiction: he indicates to his readers 1. that the manuscript presented here is the rough translation, worked over by him for the 'sheer delight of storytelling', of 2. a French book from the nineteenth century (by a certain Abbé Vallet, published in Paris in 1842) – which in the meantime has also disappeared and so cannot be checked. This in turn claims to be 3. the French edition of a book by a historian named Dom

J.Mabillon from the seventeenth century. In turn Mabillon's book presents the faithful reproduction of 4. a fourteenth-century manuscript which was written by a certain Father Adso from the famous Austrian monastery of Melk on the Danube. Here Adso of Melk tells the story of his experiences during his years as a novice at the beginning of the fourteenth century, in that very monastery on the slopes of the Apennines as a pupil of William of Baskerville.

So what do we have here? Reality or pure fantasy, facts or pure fiction, truth or deception? Who really 'guarantees' the authenticity of all these events? Anyone who asks these questions has already been trapped by this work of art. For a hovering between 'truth' and 'invention', reality and deception is of the very 'essence' of this novel – as we shall see. What reality 'really' is, how 'truth' can and cannot be known by human beings – all this is at stake in this book. The 'disguises' adopted by this twentieth-century narrator are thus an expression of the basic philosophical premise of the novel, that reality is always evasive if one tries to 'grasp' it. But in the meanwhile the reader has become much too curious about the allegedly so terrifying events and mysteries in this monastery to ponder long on the question what is true in this story and who really guarantees its authenticity. What is already mysterious is that a blind man should be the guardian of a library, an illiterate should be master of the books. What does all this mean?

In short, externally this novel is about clearing up crimes which have been committed before and during the presence in this monastery of the two main figures: the narrator Adso of Melk and the one who clears them up, the English Franciscan father William of Baskerville. In the case of the figure of William in particular Eco proves to be a particularly 'frolicsome' narrator. For with evident pleasure in this transparent game of hide and seek Eco has fused three traditions in this figure:

1. The Franciscan tradition and its opposition to a church of power and splendour which seems completely to have betrayed discipleship of the poor and powerless Christ and which can establish the truth only with the help of power (the Inquisition). (His counterpart is the Inquisitor Bernard Gui, who is the Pope's representative);

2. The philosophical tradition. Behind the English Franciscan of the novel is the Franciscan Oxford philosopher William of Ockham (c.1285-1347) and his epistemological criticism known as nominalism (the universals are nothing but 'signs' which have no reality outside the human soul) and the story of his conflict with Pope John XXII of Avignon. In 1324 he was accused of heresy in Avignon, in 1328 he fled with Michael of Casena, the general of the order, from Avignon to the Emperor Ludwig in Pisa, and later to Munich; he was the intellectual spearhead against the Pope;

3. The tradition of the detective story, since the name Baskerville is an allusion to a detective story by the Scotsman Arthur Conan Doyle (1859-1930) entitled *The Hound of the Baskervilles* (1902), his famous detective Sherlock Holmes and thus the tradition of discovering the truth by means of rational deductions from given 'signs', in detective stories called 'clues'. Moreover William of Baskerville puts himself in this tradition right at the beginning of the novel by his sharp observation of the 'signs' and his correct classification (i.e. interpretation) of them; with the help of deductive thought he can distinguish truth from error, reality from illusion. But William will not remain the sovereign epistemological figure in the course of the novel...

'Christ never laughed'

And what role does laughter play in all this? Remarkably, at William's very first meeting with old Jorge in the scriptorium of the library, where the monks are illustrating or copying the precious manuscripts, the old Spaniard vigorously censures all who cannot suppress laughter. For certain monks amused themselves by decorating manuscripts with signs of a 'perverse world', with marvellous riddles, puzzle pictures, reverse effects:

Little bird-feet heads, animals with human hands on their back, hirsute pates from which feet sprout, zebra-striped dragons, quadrupeds with serpentine necks twisted in a thousand inextricable knots, monkeys with stags' horns, sirens in the form of fowl with membranous wings, armless men with other human bodies emerging from their backs like humps, and figures with tooth-filled mouths on the belly, humans with horses' heads, and horses with human legs, fish with birds' wings and birds with fishtails, monsters with single bodies and double heads or single heads and double bodies, cows with cocks' tails and butterfly wings, women with heads scaly as a fish's back, two-headed chimeras interlaced with dragonflies with lizard snouts, centaurs, dragons, elephants, manticores stretched out on tree branches, gryphons whose tails turned into an archer in battle array, diabolical creatures with endless necks, sequences of anthropomorphic animals and zoomorphic dwarfs...[40]

Truly these were figures of a perverse world, figures to laugh at, which were there to 'comment' on the sacred texts.

But the old man has seen through this laughter and engages in an angry outburst about the laxity of his monks. When William objects by way of mitigation, 'Marginal images often provoke smiles, but to edifying ends,' the old man mocks, 'Ah yes, any image is good for inspiring virtue, provided the masterpiece of creation, turned with his head down, becomes the subject of laughter. And so the word of God is illustrated by the ass playing a lyre, the owl ploughing with a shield, oxen yoking themselves to the plough, rivers flowing upstream, the sea catching fire, the wolf turning hermit... What is the aim of this nonsense? A world that is the reverse and the opposite of that established by God, under the pretext of teaching divine precepts!'[41] And playing his last trump, the old man finally says: 'Our Lord did not have to employ such foolish things to point out the strait and narrow path to us. Nothing in his parables arouses laughter, or fear.'[42] And later still, 'John Chrysostom said that Christ never laughed.'[43]

And so it goes on in this book. The old man's fight against laughter intensifies to become a fantastic madness which makes him a murderer for God's sake. Some of the mysterious deaths are to be set to his account. Why? Because this monk wants to prevent the discovery of the book which we discussed at length in the previous chapter, the second book of Aristotle's *Poetics*, on comedy, which hitherto had been regarded in Christianity as lost.

Miracle upon miracle: in this library the only still extant copy in the West had been preserved! And the only person who knew about it was Jorge, though his own helpers had tumbled to the fact. And to prevent them from reading this book Jorge had had its pages steeped in poison, so that the curious monks immediately had to pay for the poisoning of their spirit with the poisoning of their body. Moreover this had been the cause of several deaths.

But why expend so much criminal energy on a book on laughter? Because at this time Aristotle was not just anyone. At the beginning of the fourteenth century (when Thomas Aquinas, the greatest recipient of Aristotle in the West had already been dead for more than fifty years[44]), Aristotle was already *the* authority for Christianity. And if this authority had devoted a whole book to laughter, then laughter could not be morally reprehensible! Would that not have removed the ground from any church denunciation of laughter?

Indeed, that is precisely what the old man in monk's garb, the guardian of the library, feared: his blindness is only the symbol of the fact that for this monk the truth of the church is fixed once and for all, and does not need further books, above all those which could be a danger to this truth. So Jorge preferred to refer to a church father like John Chrysostom ('Christ never laughed') against Aristotle. That is why he so passionately insisted: 'Our Lord Jesus never told comedies or fables, but only clear parables which allegorically instruct us on how to win paradise, and so be it.'[45]

Laughter as doubting the truth

So it was not just aesthetic reasons which had led this monk to combat laughter: 'Laughter shakes the body, distorts the features of the face, makes man similar to the monkey.'[46] It was not just psychological and moral reasons which made him suspect laughter. 'Laughter is a sign of foolishness. He who laughs does not believe in what he laughs at, but neither does he hate it. Therefore, laughing at evil means not preparing oneself to combat it, and laughing at good means denying the power through which good is self-propagating.'[47]

The deepest reason why this monk hated laughter lies in his anxiety about doubt: 'The spirit is serene only when it contemplates the truth and takes delight in good achieved, and truth and good are not to be laughed at. This is why Christ did not laugh. Laughter foments doubt,'[48] a doubt which is indifferent about good and evil and ultimately puts in question the very existence of God.

So what if the second book of Aristotle's *Poetics* had become known? Then laughter would be an important matter! Then laughter would no longer be morally ambiguous because it could (*horrible dictu*) serve the truth as a vehicle – through wit and word-play. Did not Aristotle write precisely this in his book on comedy? Indeed, Eco writes as though not only his Jorge but also his William had in fact laid hands on the book which had disappeared. And thanks to Eco we respectful readers are witnesses of a unique scene: the first reading in the world of a book by Aristotle which had previously vanished.

This is how it happens. At the end of the novel William has caught on to the old man. They meet for a last great dispute in that forbidden library in which William has at last tracked down the book of death. The old man still believes that William, too, has fallen into the poison trap. But he has wisely protected his hands with gloves. And so he can now read it – simultaneously translating the Greek original into Latin:

In the first book we dealt with tragedy and saw how, by arousing pity and fear, it produces catharasis, the purification of those feelings. As we promised, we will now deal with comedy (as well as with satire and mime) and see how, in inspiring the pleasure of the ridiculous, it arrives at the purification of that passion. That such passion is most worthy of consideration we have already said in the book on the soul, inasmuch as – alone among the animals – man is capable of laughter. We will then define the type of actions of which comedy is the mimesis, then we will examine the means by which comedy excites laughter, and these means are action and speech. We will show how the ridiculousness of actions is born from the likening of the best to the worst and vice versa, from arousing surprise through deceit, from the impossible, from violation of the laws of nature, from the irrelevant and the inconsequent, from the debasing of the characters, from the use of comical and vulgar pantomime, from disharmony, from the choice of the less worthy things. We will then show how the ridiculousness of speech is born from the misundertandings of similar words for different things and different words for similar things, from garrulity and repetition, from play on words, from diminutives, from errors of pronunciation, and from barbarisms...[49]

With that the reading breaks off, and Aristotle returns to silence. We readers of the twentieth century are confronted once and for all with two ways of seeing laughter, two ways which clash fatally in Eco's novel. Fatally, because laughter is not harmless but literally involves everything, being or not being, truth or lie, God's order or the devil's chaos. On the one hand there is the way of Aristotle, the way of the functional affirmation of laughter, which William of Baskerville takes up and intensifies, laughter in the interest of knowing the truth: 'Aristotle sees the tendency to laughter as a force for good, which can also have an instructive value: through witty riddle and unexpected metaphors, though it tells us things differently from the way they are, as if it were lying, it actually obliges us to examine them more closely, and it makes us say: ah, this is just how things are, and I didn't know it. Truth reached by depicting men and the world as worse than they are or than we believe them to be, worse in any case than the epics, the tragedies, lives of the saints have shown them to us.'[50]

And on the other hand there is the anxiety of the Christian monk that as a result of the distortions, deceptions and lies prompted by laughter the truth will no longer be distinguishable from the lie, certainty from delusion, good from evil, God from the devil. Here is laughter not as an instrument for discovering the truth but as an expression of the loss of truth, the denial of the truth. Here is laughter not as part of an ultimately ordered world but as the expression of a world which has gone wrong and become perverted, a world in which not only religion and morality but also politics and society have been turned upside down. For with the loss of the moral order has not also the social order been lost? Does not the loss of religious truth ultimately also lead to the loss of the moral and political order?

Laughter as subversion and liberation from anxiety

Because all this is at stake, the moral and political order, the old monk cannot be indifferent to laughter. And so in the tower of the library at the climax of the argument he vents all his contempt on his adversary William. We must document this great key passage in full; to bring out the most important points better I have put them in italics.

Laughter is weakness, corruption, the foolishness of our flesh. It is the peasant's entertainment, the drunkard's licence; even the church in her wisdom has granted the moment of feast, carnival, fair, this diurnal pollution that releases humours and distracts from other desires and other ambitions... Still, *laughter remains base*, a defence for the simple, a mystery desecrated for the plebeians. The apostle also said as much: it is better to marry than to burn. Rather than rebel against God's established order, laugh and enjoy your foul parodies of order, at the end of the meal, after you have drained jugs and flasks. Elect the king of fools, lose yourselves in the liturgy of the ass and pig, play at performing your saturnalia head down...

But here, *here* [the reference is to the book by Aristotle] the function of laughter is reversed, it is *elevated to art*, the doors of the world of the learned are opened to it, it becomes the object of philosophy, and of perfidous theology... Laughter frees the villein from fear of the Devil, because in the feast of fools the Devil also appears poor and foolish, and therefore controllable. But this book could teach that *freeing oneself of the fear* of the Devil is wisdom. When he laughs, as the wine gurgles in his throat, the villein feels he is master, because he has overturned his position with respect to his lord; but this book could teach learned men the clever and, from that moment, illustrious artifices that could *legitimatize the reversal*. Then what in the villein is still, fortunately, an operation of the belly would be transformed into an operation of the brain. That laughter is proper to man is a sign of our limitation, sinners that we are. But from this book many corrupt minds like yours would draw the extreme syllogism, whereby *laughter is man's end*! Laughter, for a few moments, distracts the villein from fear. But law is imposed by fear, whose true name is fear of God. This book could strike the *Luciferine spark* that would set a new fire to the whole world, and laughter would be defined as the new art, unknown even to Prometheus, for cancelling fear. To the villein who laughs, at that moment dying does not matter; but then, when the licence is past, the liturgy again imposes on him, according to the divine plan, the fear of death. And from this book there could be born the new destructive aim *to destroy death through redemption from fear*. And what would we be, we sinful creatures, without fear, perhaps the most foresighted, the most loving of the divine gifts?... A Greek philosopher (whom your Aristotle quotes here, an accomplice and foul *auctoritas*) said that the seriousness of opponents must be dispelled with laughter, and laughter opposed with seriousness. The prudence of our fathers made its choice: if laughter is the *delight of the plebeians*, the licence of the plebeians must be restrained and humiliated, and intimidated by sternness. And the plebeians have no weapons for refining their laughter until they have made it an instrument against the seriousness of the spiritual shepherds who must lead them to eternal life and rescue them from the seductions of belly, pudenda, food, their sordid desires. But if one day somebody, brandishing the words of the Philosopher and thus speaking as a philosopher, were to raise the art of laughter to the condition of subtle weapon, if the rhetoric of conviction were to be replaced by the rhetoric of mockery, if the topic of the patient construction of the images of redemption were to be replaced by the *topic of the impatient dismantling and upsetting* of every holy and venerable image – oh, that day even you, William, and all your knowledge, would be swept away!'[51]

This is indeed the key passage for our question. For Eco has put into the mouth of his mediaeval figure the essential insights of present-day psychology and sociology of laughter.

1. Laughter is the *rechannelling of aggression*. As such it can be allowed by the rulers for psychological relief (purification and diversion) and social relief (laughter as a prophylactic against revolution). This function of laughter can be used even by the church, as laughter in this sense is the 'lesser evil' – following the maxim that it is better to laugh at the divinely willed order for a while than to want to change it. In this perspective festivals, carnivals, annual fairs have a function in stabilizing society. They are a psychological ventilation which is allowed temporarily and is useful. An allusion to the famous book by the Russian literary critic Mikhail Bakhtin on the subversive power of the mediaeval popular culture of laughter (directed against the feudal laws and

the church hierarchy) entitled *Literature and Carnival* (1969) is unmistakable here.

2. Laughter is a new art form, the supreme consummation of human beings: the *liberation of the Luciferine spark*. In such laughter human beings become masters of their own fate. They begin to control themselves. Now if human beings control their fate they detach themselves from situations of domination; they rebel, attempt rebellion, tear down the barriers between classes. The servant no longer remains the servant.

3. Political liberation is matched by psychological liberation. The art of laughter is *at the same time the art of annihilating anxiety*. Where does the annihilation of anxiety lead? It leads to the annihilation of death! And where does the annihilation of death lead? It leads to the abandonment of belief in redemption, to the abolition of any binding truth. Human laughter, the 'rhetoric of mockery', if pursued consistently, leads to a loss of the function of the church, indeed to the abolition of God.

How are we to understand all this? In what wider context is it to be put? The term 'postmodern' is often used in the interpretation of Eco's work. Is there a connection between the theme of laughter and the diagnosis of postmodernity? If so, what is it?

5. Laughter as the Signature of 'Postmodernity'

'Postmodern' is in fact nowadays the word most frequently used in intellectual circles in criticism of our time and culture. It is as popular as it is disputed.

What is 'postmodern'?

If we survey the wide-ranging discussion, three typical directions emerge, each of which pursues its own interests with this word:

1. Some, above all in the sphere of German and American theology (H.Küng, D.R.Griffin[52]), associate with 'postmodernity' a description of new basic human attitudes to the symptoms of crisis in our time which point towards the future (on ecology, partnership, world peace, the world ecumene). The destructive forces of modernity ('the dialectic of the Enlightenment') are seen through and are regarded as being there to be conquered. The

'project of modernity' with its human and Enlightenment potential is not rejected, but is developed further dialectically. According to this concept, 'postmodernity' is understood as a 'sublation' of modernity in the threefold Hegelian sense: affirmation of its humane content, negation of its inhumane limits and the transcending of modernity in the direction of a new, differentiated, pluralistic and holistic synthesis.

2. Others, above all in the sphere of German philosophy and theology (J.Habermas, J.B.Metz[53]), associate with 'postmodernity' a reactionary antimodernity or a radical pluralism negating all binding values, which in the epistemological sphere radically denies that there is a single truth and in the ethical sphere radically denies that there are universal, generally binding criteria and values. So according to the most recent diagnosis by Johann Baptist Metz the moral climate in Europe fluctuates 'between the declared will for moral suspension generally and "petty morality" of a postmodern kind'. What constitutes the 'postmodernity' of this morality? Metz argues that it is 'morality with diminished and movable criteria, with a renunciation of all too long-term, indeed lifelong loyalties, with the proviso of self realization in any risk, with an insistence on the right to reverse any commitment, but also quite generally a morality which individualizes all conflicts, is indifferent to a wide consensus, and suspects all universalistic terms'.[54]

3. What certain philosophers and theologians find repulsive about 'postmodernity', philosophical theoreticians especially in France (R.F.Barthes, J.F.Lyotard[55]) or cultural critics in the United States (L.Fielder[56]) find particularly fascinating: the dissolution of all previous patterns of thought, writing and life and the regaining of the greatest possible plurality of contents, styles, cultures and languages, both synchronous (the awareness of a global contemporaneity) and diachronous (the awareness of a historical contemporaneity). The fact that 'postmodernity' is available to all means that nothing (whether moral or cultural, social or intellectual) is tabu, and sets off a move towards freedom in the sphere of art. Art becomes the amusing play of all with all, including ambivalences which are deliberately set up and labyrinths of meaning which are artificially created.

And what is a 'postmodern' work of art? It is a collage of random themes, forms, procedures and languages, of deliberately calculated openness and freedom (quotations ranging from world literature to trivial literature). And the 'postmodern' author? He or she is the witty arranger of realities, who at the same time deceives and disappoints, the master or mistress of disguise and disclosure, the one who plays with facticity and fiction, seriousness and parody, staging and ironic transcendence, indeed lies and truth. And what about 'postmodern' literary texts? They are the results of intertextuality, i.e. an arranged interplay of old and new, familiar and invented texts from the *Divine Comedy* to the comic strip.

'Postmodern' aesthetics: play – irony – masquerade

One representative of this third trend in the sphere of aesthetics is Umberto Eco, the professor of 'semiotics' who himself once called his 'theory of signs' a theory of lies.[57] For Eco, 'postmodernity' is not the designation of an epoch or a political or moral disposition of the mind but purely and artistically 'a way of operating, an artistic concern'.[58] Just as every epoch has had its mannerism, so too each has its own postmodernity which arises out of moments of crisis. Why? For Eco, if the past becomes too strong, burdens and oppresses everything, then a need for freedom develops: for the destruction and overcoming of the old and for new experiences and forms of expression. In this way the avant-garde arises in the sphere of art, just as the avant-garde of modernity arose at the end of the previous century. 'The avant-garde destroys, defaces the past: *Les Demoiselles d'Avignon* is a typical avant-garde act. Then the avant-garde goes further, destroys the figure, cancels it, it arrives at the abstract, the informal, the white canvas, the slashed canvas, the charred canvas. In architecture and the visual arts it will be the curtain wall, the building as steel, pure parallelepiped, minimal art; in literature, the destruction of the flow of discourse, the Burroughs-like collage, silence, the white page; in music, the passage from atonality to noise to absolute silence (in this sense, the early Cage is modern).'[59]

And today? Today, according to Eco, it is again time for a new shift. The avant-garde of modernity has worn itself out, has become 'classic' in its time; its codes are empty. Here postmodernity comes into play: 'The postmodern reply to the modern consists of recognizing that the past, since it cannot really be destroyed, because its destruction leads to silence, must be revisited; but with irony, not innocently...irony, metalinguistic play, enunciation squared.'[60]

In his novel *The Name of the Rose* Eco has engaged in a practical experiment by means of a theoretical example. For what is this novel if not an expression of irony, metalinguistic play and enunciation 'squared'? The play on names, persons and events is already ironical; so too is the play on the genre of the detective story, the fourfold manuscript fiction created right at the start, the threefold beginning of the novel: the report by the author Eco of the manuscripts he claims have been found; the report by Adso in his old age on the presuppositions of his story ('prologue') and the real experiences of the young Adso in the uncanny monastery. That is ironic intertextuality to the full, but each of these beginnings takes up literary traditions on which there is a play here: the literary-historical (the identification of the manuscript), the theological-philosophical (the monastery life, church history, theological dispute) and the elements of trivial literature: 'It was a beautiful morning at the end of November' – so the novel begins. The natural scientist Teresa de Lauretis, who interpreted Eco's work as a postmodern novel at a very early stage, is therefore right in saying: 'It is a text which is almost completely made up of other texts, of stories which have already been told once, of names which are either known to us, or sound as if they must really be known to us, from the history of literature and culture. It is a text which presents a potpourri of famous passages and obscure quotations and which collects together a technical vocabulary, many sub-codes (narrative, iconographic, literary, architectural, bibliographical, pharmaceutical, etc.) and finally figures which seem to have been taken from a universal encyclo-paedia.'[61]

However, all this is consistent for Eco only if it corresponds to the basic philosophical premises of his own discipline, 'semiotics'. For semiotics investigates and formulates the origin and use of signs, in which anything in the world can become a 'sign': a thing or an expression, a noise or a clue or an idea. Certainly the significance of this sign or the relationship between the signs can be established by rules of interpretation, but in principle the connection between the signs is completely open. Indeed the wealth of signs allows an infinite multiplicity of associations and interpretations. Here the insight is taken seriously that knowledge, even scientific knowledge, is never absolute, always fallible, is used in a continuum of uncertainty and indeterminacy. Therefore, 'For semiotics as a science which formally describes the use of signs, all cultures, world views, texts and works of art are as equal as the citizen before the law. Semiotics as a metascience produces a universal suprahistorical capacity for making a connection between all cultural phenomena. Historical differences are no longer insurmountable limits, but meanings among others. So one can shift the modern genre of the detective story to the Middle Ages or tell the history of the critique of reason as a penny dreadful.'[62]

Now semiotics is not only the science above all sciences; by its intellectual cut it is also the sympathetic expression of what one can call 'postmodernity' in the third sense, which is critical of culture. For the theory of signs lives by its insight into the impossibility of insights in principle; its significance is that it produces an awareness of an ultimate meaninglessness of all signs; its truth is the description of the fact that there can be no absolute truth for human beings.

And because that is the case, because semiotics is a 'theory of lies', because the work of art seeks to be an act of deliberate deception of its viewer or reader and the artist is a counterfeiter, because the order of things is always only apparent, provisional, still not given, then the poetics of postmodernity can also be described as a poetics of deliberate voluntariness, of the calculated beautiful appearance which presents itself as appearance. In short, because that is the case, the poetics of postmodernity is the poetics of the 'as if', a wink of the eye and agreement over the degree of deception which one will accept.

It is not far from here to laughter. For if the poetics of postmodernity is a poetics of play, of masquerade and irony 'squared', of contentment and amusement, then this poetics corresponds to an aesthetic of laughter: laughter at the fact that one is free from all binding ties, values and norms, that one stands 'above' everything and regards the world as one's own material for play. If nothing is binding any more and everything is fluid, if the 'as if' reigns, then in fact laughter can be a congenial expression of this poetics. Laughter is the objective correlate of the spirit or demon of 'postmodernity' defined in this way.[63]

What is left: laugh or be silent

And precisely that is what Eco's *Rose* novel is also steering towards. For its main character, William of Baskerville, undergoes a remarkable conversion: a conversion from 'modern' certainty (sure knowledge of the truth with the aid of rational deduction) to postmodern uncertainty. Paradoxically, the blind fanatic Jorge had proved to be clear-sighted at this particular point. For in the last great duel of speeches between the two he had virtually told William to his face that if he tolerated laughter he himself would finally get caught up in the whirlpool. He would conclude from Aristotle that 'the supreme consummation of man lies in laughter'! Laughter – the 'new art', the 'art of the annihilation of anxiety'! Laughter as an expression of the denial of a binding order and truth, as a denial of the existence of God? And that is precisely what happens: William, the representative of rationality and intellect, of empiricism and enlightenment, in the end finds himself deceived despite his success.

Certainly William had discovered the truth about the murders, but to some degree only 'by chance'. All the clues he discovered in which he thought that he had detected the great plan of a criminal mastermind had proved to be deceptive: not all the murders had the same cause; many events were linked only by a complicated chain of causes. And William had wrongly understood all the 'signs' which indicated an apocalyptic divine judgment; they had been deliberately 'staged' later by Jorge. William had certainly found out the truth, but not through his own rational deduction as he thought and hoped: it had 'happened' to him. His reconstruction of reality with the help of allegedly indubitable signs, his belief in an ultimate order and truth accessible to rational thought, proved to be self-deception. The truth revealed itself as a product of chance; it was recognized 'by mistake'... So here too there is a refined effect of reversal in the novel: the one who enlightens is in the end the one who is deceived, the one who is blind in the end again becomes the seer.

But how does William of Baskerville now react to the shattering of his capacity for knowledge? He concedes to his pupil: 'Perhaps the mission of those who love mankind is to make people laugh at the truth, to make truth laugh, because the only truth lies in learning to free ourselves from insane passion for the truth.'[64]

How is this passage to be understood? Because of its fundamental significance for the general statement of the construction of the novel we must interpret the text which follows (the closing pages of the internal action) sentence by sentence. So what does William mean by his recognition that the only truth is to free oneself from an 'insane passion' for the truth? Does he mean by this liberation only from the insane form of the certainty of truth embodied in this novel by Jorge and the Inquisitor? Is William's concern the removal of fantasy? Or more? Is it the insight that there is something insane about any certainty about the truth and that laughter 'about' alleged human truth is the only appropriate measure? The further course of the conversation suggests that the second, more radical, option is the more probable. For in the subsequent conversation with his pupil William makes objections to the overall order of the world:

1. William does not dispute that there are 'signs of truth', true things, incontrovertible facts (Jorge is a murderer, Aristotle is the author of the sought-after book). The difference comes earlier: William doubts the possibility of ever understanding the 'reciprocal relationship between the signs'. So he sought a single author of all the crimes, but in the end had to discover that basically each crime had a different author or – in the case of a suicide, no author at all.

2. From this impossibility of recognizing the reciprocal influence between the signs, William now concludes that 'there is no order in the universe'.[65] There is only the order that the human spirit imagines. And according to William this order is 'like a net or a ladder, built to attain something. But once one has attained it, one must "throw it away", since it is evident that while it was useful, it makes no sense. "*Er muoz gelichesame die leiter abewerfen, sô er an ir ufgestigen*".'[66] This quotation, which is apparently in Middle High German (allegedly from a mystic from Adso's homeland, Austria), proves on closer inspection to be a subtly disguised quotation from the history of twentieth-century philosophy. It indeed comes from a 'mystic' from Adso's homeland, Austria, from Ludwig Wittgenstein, who at the end of his famous

Tractatus Logico-Philosophicus (which was published in 1921), used the image of the ladder: 'My propositions are elucidatory in this way: he who understands me finally recognizes them as senseless, when he has climbed out through them, on them, over them. (He must so to speak throw away the ladder, after he has climbed up on it.) He must surmount these propositions; then he sees the world rightly. Whereof one cannot speak, thereof one must be silent.'[67]

3. But there is a deep theological reason why for William there is all at once no order in the world; in other words, it is connected with his understanding of God: with God's free will and God's omnipotence, a key notion of the philosopher and theologian William of Ockham, as whose mask William of Baskerville is in fact conceived. So God's omnipotence and free will prevent an order in the world, for such an order would 'offend the free will of God and his omnipotence'. It follows from this: 'So the freedom of God is our condemnation.' But William adds another clause, 'or at least the condemnation of our pride'.[68]

However, with this last sentence William gives his argument yet another double meaning. What is he getting at? With the reference to God's free will and omnipotence is he pointing to a humiliation of man – by the slogan, God's order exists, but it is not given to human beings to understand it? Or to more? Is God's alleged order not order at all, but *a priori* chaos, because it is the expression of an arbitrary omnipotence of God, so that God's freedom indeed would become 'our condmnenation'?

Moreover the question put by Adso, witness to these last insights of the master, points in this direction: 'But how can a necessary being exist totally polluted with the possible? What difference is there, then, between God and primigenial chaos? Isn't affirming God's absolute omnipotence and His absolute freedom with regard to His own choices tantamount to demonstrating that God does not exist?'[69] But again William answers only cryptically, more evasively, as if he himself did not want to draw the last consequences. He says only: 'How could a learned man go on communicating his learning if he answered yes to your question?'[70] So William still seems to be holding to the connection between God's existence and trusting in the possibility of communicating knowledge. But to become completely clear, Adso asks once again: 'Do you mean that there would be no possible and communicable learning any more if the very criterion of truth were lacking, or do you mean you could no longer communicate what you know because others would not allow you to?'[71]

But this last question of Adso's remains unanswered once and for all, since at this moment the monastery collapses in a blazing inferno. William can only murmur to himself, 'There is too much confusion here', and thus draw a negative conclusion, '*Non in commotione Dominus*', which means something like, 'The Lord is not in the commotion, not in the uproar.' This is William's last word, since shortly afterwards Adso finally parts from his master. But these closing words accord completely with the basic philosophical premises of the inner treatment of the novel. In the last questions there is no answer, at any rate no answer which would make the questions about truth, God, order, the capacity to know disappear. The last questions remain unanswered and the truly last question is the question of the basic criterion of truth, and of the guarantee that what human beings know also corresponds to the truth. Only the vague hope remains that God the Lord may not be in the 'commotion', in the 'chaos'.

However, these philosophical premises of the inner action are modified yet again by the external action. For the position of the inner action (William) is by no means identical with that of the external action (Adso). Grown old, Adso draws the consequences which William evidently still wanted to evade. As an old man, constantly reflecting on his story, Adso comes to the even more radical conviction, critical of the truth, which is not to be found in William in this form. The events in the monastery are nothing but 'a product of chance' and contain 'no message'.[72] The world? It has become a dance of death, a house of fools: 'Where are the snows of yesteryear? The earth is dancing the dance of Macabre: at times it seems to me that the Danube is crowded with ships loaded with fools going toward a dark place.'[73]

What remains? For Adso, what remains is not laughter, as it is for William, but mystical silence:

> All I can do is be silent...Soon I shall be joined with my beginning, and I no longer believe that it is the God of glory of whom the abbots of my order spoke to me, or of joy, as the Minorites believed in those days, perhaps not even of piety.

God is a *lauter Nichts, ihn rührt kein Nun noch Hier...* I shall soon enter this broad desert, perfectly level and boundless, where the truly pious heart succumbs in bliss. I shall sink into the divine shadow, in a dumb silence and an ineffable union, and in this sinking all equality and all inequality shall be lost, and in that abyss my spirit will lose itself, and will not know the equal or the unequal, or anything else: and all differences will be forgotten. I shall be in the simple foundation, in the silent desert where diversity is never seen, in the privacy where no one finds himself in his proper place. I shall fall into the silent and uninhabited divinity where there is no work and no image...[74]

That makes it clear that William and Adso embody two different consequences of the same experiences of the chaos of the signs of the word. Eco himself has described these differences like this: 'Adso was very important for me. From the outset I wanted to tell the whole story (with its mysteries, its political and theological events, its ambiguities) through the voice of someone who experiences the events, records them all with the photographic fidelity of an adolescent but does not understand them (and will not understand them fully even as an old man, since he then chooses a flight into the divine nothingness, which was not what his mother had taught him) to make everything understood through the words of one who understands nothing.'[75]

Does this mean that Eco as author is to be found on the side of the 'master'? Is not his message for the twentieth-century reader identical with that of William? Is there then a message from the author in all the messages of the novel, a position in all the positions? No, this play with the sympathies for a fictitious creature is also part of the aesthetic programme. Through his subtle multiplicity of layers and references the author has confronted his readers with options without anticipating decisions, closing ways out. He remains concealed behind all the figures, much as he may sympathize with one or the other. In so doing he performs the task of a great work of art: to draw the reader into basic decisions about the state of the world, to entangle the reader in complex discussions about the signs of reality, without himself laying down meaning at the level of the novel or even answering the question of the truth. Eco's novel is a deliberately calculated labyrinth of meaning, and the reader needs to be careful about getting into this labyrinth.[76]

After all this we can no longer overlook the fact that this book contains a theological provocation of far-reaching radicalism. Have human beings to learn under the sign of 'postmodernity' to liberate themselves from the truth, because the 'signs' are now impossible to interpret and therefore there is something insane about any claim to truth? Is laughter 'about' the truth the only possibility for human beings of being able to live in the world of postmodernity? So in the end is there nothing but the postmodern contentment with reading, the poetics of the uncommitted and the calculated appearance which is in love with itself and at the same time ironical? That is the challenge of the internal action. The challenge of the external action is even more radical: silence, mystical darkness as the last refuge for the person who has lost the order of the world.

As far as I can see, very few theologians have gone to the trouble of taking the basic philosophical and theological premises of this novel really seriously – which is amazing given the enormous influence of the book worldwide.[77] One takes Eco seriously only if one takes seriously the question of truth, knowledge and certainty, of revelation and God, in short everything that is hidden behind the complex of 'laughter'. After being instructed by the following chapters, we shall return once again to this challenge of Eco's at the end of this 'Brief Theology of Laughter'.

II

Human Laughter and God's Laughter –
A Biblical Tableau

1. The Christian Condemnation of Laughter

'Christ never laughed'! The fictitious dispute in Eco's mediaeval novel is more than fiction. It reflects a line of tradition which really existed, from John Chrysostom through Augustine to Bernard of Clairvaux and Hugo of St Victor, of the Christian denunciation of laughter, above all in monastic circles in the Middle Ages.

Despised laughter: church fathers and monks

Of course the Christian Middle Ages also knew a culture of laughter. The Russian literary critic Mikhail Bakhtin, whom I have already mentioned, spoke of a 'carnivalistic sense of the world' specifically in the Middle Ages. By this we are to understand a readiness to put any meaning whatever in question, continually to caricature and attack a spiritual unworldliness with a stress on the material-sensual and the crudely-physical.

In the grotesqueness of the carnival people gave themselves space against political and ecclesiastical legalization. The carnival sense of the world was a counter to the contemporary strict religious conceptions of order, opposition to the regimentation imposed by the spiritual and worldly powers, insisting on seriousness and thus immutability, rebellion against the intimidating rituals of the church, an overcoming of cosmic anxiety.[1]

Certainly today we must largely relativize this attractive theory of Bakhtin's, because his scheme with its Marxist sociological stamp (on the one hand the humourless feudal lords and hierarchies, on the other the people delighting in mockery and laughter) cannot be maintained: on closer inspection there are

43

many panegyrics of laughter and many presentations of comedy in Latin, 'the language of domination', and in any case the upper classes had more freedom to enjoy comedy than the people, who were often condemned to dull earnestness.[2] But beyond doubt in the Middle Ages there was the view of the world described by Bakhtin, 'which put in question everything, including everything that was ordered, polished, indeed hallowed, by recalling the chaotic, material and physical side of life, in grotesque physical images with overdrawn signals of fertility, in the vital substances of the sexual which are at least temporarily suppressed by all civilization, in crudeness of words and actions, in blatant smut'.[3]

Conversely, we must not overlook the fact that in mediaeval monastic circles there was precisely the opposite tendnecy. If we follow the studies of the Tübingen historian Gerhard Schmitz, we can see that at any rate in mediaeval monasticism laughter 'was not a positive value; on the contrary, it was a non-value. Weeping was valuable, laughter was contemptible.'[4] So in principle laughter was regarded as offensive and undignified, since it was part of monastic self-control that the monk never laughed. That emerges above all from the widely circulated monastic rule of St Benedict (who died c.547), in which any trivial gossip of monks tending to laughter was forbidden. Frequent and loud laughter, jokes and idle words prompting laughter were to be suppressed. As a degree of humility it was held that one should not laugh lightly and suddenly; this was justified by a proverb that only the fool bursts out laughing.

The same is true of the earliest commentary on the Rule of Benedict which has come down to us. Here too we can learn that it is more appropriate for the monk to weep than to laugh, since we live 'in a vale of tears'. So monks might not laugh, but had to mourn: 'We must shed tears for our sins, tears for the weakness of the body, tears of longing for our creator and communion with the angels and saints, tears that we may be preserved from the punishments of hell and the snares of the devil.' And what is the theological basis for this? In addition to quotations from scripture, all of which do not favour laughter (Proverbs 14.13; Ecclesiastes 7.4; Sirach 21.15, 20), reference is made above all to the example of Christ. We know that while Christ often wept, he never laughed.

Here mediaeval monasticism could appeal to the basic convictions of certain church fathers. Here they already found a climate of pessimism about the world which fitted in with their own experiences. The world is transitory, human beings are mortal, the creation is a *valis lacrimarum*, a vale of tears. Laughter is at best reserved for the next world. So Jerome (c.347-419/20) can write: 'As long as we are in the vale of tears we may not laugh, but must weep. So the Lord also says, "Blessed are those who weep, for they shall laugh." We are in the vale of tears and this age is one of tears, not of joy.'[5] And for the greatest theologian of the Latin church, Aurelius Augustine (354-430), human life is also full of misery, work, pain, anger, tribulation and temptation. Certainly Augustine also knows that human beings have a capacity to laugh which distinguishes them from animals, but he completely devalues this distinction: 'Human beings laugh and weep, and it is a matter for weeping that they laugh!'[6]

The theology of tears

Let us cast a brief glance at this world and look up the passage which Eco's pious fanatic Jorge of Burgos was constantly quoting. It comes from a work of John Chrystostom (444/54-507), who was first a celebrated preacher in Antioch before he became bishop in what was then the imperial capital, Constantinople. He received the honorific name Chrysostom, 'Golden Mouth', for his rhetorical brilliance and profound pastoral ministry. More-over his main works include not only treatises of an ascetic character on monastic life and commentaries on scripture, but also numerous sermons and discourses. For a while he became an ascetic monk of his own free will (but overdid things, so that he had to give up this life on grounds of health), and he preferred to preach on practical, moral, ascetic themes. The sixth homily in his commentary on the Gospel of Matthew gives us a fine insight into this way of thinking.

Chrysostom takes a passage from the infancy narrative in the Gospel of Matthew as the occasion for an admonitory sermon with a strict ethical slant. The passage is: 'Now when Herod heard this, he was afraid, and all Jerusalem with him' (Matt.2.3). Here John is discussing 'all Jerusalem' 'being afraid'. He wants to detect as much of this fear in his hearers as once there was in Herod. For among his audience John suspects that there are all kinds of 'vices': indifference, laziness, a lack of spiritual fire. He is evidently dealing with a Christianity which has become comfortable and middle-class, and no longer betrays anything of the original great Christian ideals.

What is the alternative? John argues that one must be seized with 'love', and then one can give away all one's possessions, despise wealth and places of honour, indeed even sacrifice one's life: 'For the warmth of that fire entering into the soul casts out all sluggishness, and makes him whom it has seized lighter than anything that soars; and thenceforth overlooking the things that are seen, such a one abides in continual compunction, pouring forth never ceasing fountains of tears, and thence reaping fruit of great delight. For nothing so unites and binds to God as such tears.'[7]

Here Chrysostom has reached a decisive point, his theology of tears. And in this context we now meet the saying that interests us:

If you also weep such tears, you have become a follower of your Lord. For he too wept, both over Lazarus and over the city, and he was deeply moved over the fate of Judas. And this indeed one may often see him do, but nowhere laugh nor smile even a little; no one at least of the evangelists mentions this. Therefore also with regard to Paul, that he wept, that he did so night and day for three years, both he says of himself and others say of him; but that he laughed neither does he himself say anywhere, nor does one or other of the saints, either about him or about any other like him; but this is said of Sarah only, when she is blamed, and of the son of Noah, when for a freeman he became a slave.

I say all these things not to suppress all laughter, but to take away dissipation of mind. For tell me, why are you luxurious and dissolute while you are still responsible for such serious sins, and are to stand at a fearful judgment seat and will have to give a strict account of all that has been done here? Yes, for we are to give an account both of what we have sinned willingly, and what against our will...

Since, then, the things for which you have to give account are so great, do you sit laughing and talking wittily, and giving yourself up to luxury? 'Why,' one may say, 'if I did not do so, but mourned, what would be the profit?' Very great indeed; even so great as to be beyond expression. For while you cannot escape punishment after the sentence at a temporal tribunal, however much you weep, here you have only to annul the sentence and obtain pardon.

That is why Christ says so much to us about mourning, and blesses those who mourn, and calls those who laugh wretched. For this is not the theatre for laughter, neither did we come together for this intent, that we may give way to immoderate mirth, but that we may groan, and by this groaning inherit a kingdom.[8]

It does not take any lengthy explanations for us to understand that here mediaeval monasticism saw a prior form of its own spirituality. Certainly Chrysostom explicitly says that he does not simply want to make laughter tabu, but merely to prevent dissipation. Thus Chrysostom seems to be concerned with condemning only the extreme form of laughter – like Plato and Aristotle, the great ethicists of virtue in antiquity. The literary critic Ernst Robert Curtius, whose pioneering study on *European Literature and the Latin Middle Ages* (1948) contains a short chapter on 'The Church and Laughter', may therefore be right in observing that 'The ideal values of antiquity were taken over by early Christian monasticism'.[9]

The one who laughs as the one who is remote from God

And yet we would completely mistake the dialectic of the theology of tears if we supposed that John Chrysostom was merely combatting extreme forms of laughter. For what is decisive for him is the view that it is not laughter, but only weeping, which binds a person to God. Indeed for John the dialectic of the theology of tears evidently consists in the fact that there is a joy of weeping, a satisfaction in tears, a contentment in mourning: those who are ready to repent are the happy ones; those who are humble are the ones who please God; those who sigh will inherit heaven!

The reason for this is unambiguous: weeping alone unites with God, while laughter leads a person away from God, alienates Christians from their Creator. The model is Christ himself, who was often seen to weep but never to laugh. Or there are the apostle

Paul and the saints. How much does a woman like Sarah count here? So good Christians have no reason to be dissipated, to burst out laughing, to say silly things and devote themselves to the idle pleasures of life, since they have enough sins to repent of and have to account for themselves before the judgment seat of God. Thus in John Chrysostom we have an identification of laughter and vanity, laughter and forgetfulness of sins, indeed laughter and remoteness from God, which has a powerful effect in history.

The one who laughs is the one who is remote from God. This Christian archetype of thought has deep roots in the early church with its Hellenistic stamp. It also left a deep mark on the Middle Ages, and above all on its monasticism. So we can now understand all the better the historian's conclusion about this line of Christian tradition: 'Laughter has no positive connotations in the mediaeval doctrine of the church; it is and remains suspect and worth fighting against... Laughter, if not *a priori* sin, was at least a serious error. The theme which the mediaeval church kept striking up again and again was not enjoyment and pleasure, but contempt and the overcoming of this world, and from England to Italy, from Spain to Germany, whole libraries have been filled with treatises in which contempt for the world is praised and justified as the only adequate attitude for human beings because of their high destiny.'[10] *Indeed in the Middle Ages there was no theology of laughter, but there was a theology of tears.* So are reflections on a theology of laughter *a priori* to be judged trivial, an expression of scepticism, indeed ultimately godless? Do theological reflections on laughter fail in that moral earnestness with which one must ultimately drive out laughter? It is time to make a deeper theological investigation of laughter, and we do this best if we go back behind what the 'church fathers' say and explicitly appeal to the foundation documents of Christianity itself, the scripture to which John Chrysostom also explicitly refers. So we ask, what do the biblical documents say about laughter, if one does not read them with the eyes of the ascetic and moralist from Constantinople?

2. Human beings laugh at God: Sarah and Abraham

If we turn first to the Old, or better the First, Testament,[11] three basic motifs of laughter strike us, which we must now discuss: 1. the human being who laughs at God; 2. the God who laughs at the rulers and the wicked; and 3. the one who laughs as the 'fool', whose laughter is simply the reflection of fatal self-deception about his situation.

The laughter of doubt

One cannot get rid of Sarah as quickly as John Chrysostom thinks. For if there is any story in the First Testament with human laughter at its centre, it is the story of Abraham's wife Sarah in the book of Genesis. Let us recall the situation – leaving aside all literary-critical questions which are irrelevant in this context – as the text in its final form wanted to leave it with us. God, the Lord, appears to Abraham who is almost a hundred years old, in the grove of oaks at Mamre, in the guise of three men. Abraham learns that his wife, who has similarly grown very old and remained childless, will bring a son into the world within a year. Sarah overhears this conversation and reacts in what is psychologically a very plausible way. She laughs 'to herself', and thinks: 'After I have grown old, and my husband is old, shall I have pleasure?' (18.12). But God notices this quiet laughter and asks in rebuke: 'Why did Sarah laugh, and say "Shall I indeed bear a child, now that I am old?" Is anything too hard for the Lord? At the appointed time I will return to you, in the spring, and Sarah shall have a son' (18.3f.). Thus rebuked, Sarah suddenly denies her laughter, 'I did not laugh', and the narrator adds as the reason, 'for she was afraid' (18.15).

What is the reason for this laughter of Sarah and what form of laughter do we have here? Many tones and overtones may be detectable in this laughter: 'a touch of flirting', 'a chuckling recollection of pleasure', 'a little sorrow, unbelieving hope'.[12] All this may be detected here. But the decisive thing seems to me to be this. Sarah perceives a promise for the future, compares it with her reality and notes a discrepancy which is so great as to be comical. The probability of the promised possibility is so small that it makes her laugh. So the reason for her laughter is the experience of the contrast between reality and possibility, so that the character of the laugh is not one of perplexity or despair, but one of doubt.

Thus for all the quietness of the 'laughing to herself', Sarah's laughter must be interpreted as doubt in a future possibility, as an expression of a laughable discrepancy between human and divine potential. Sarah's laugh is a 'laugh of incredulity',[13] without conflicting with the promises. Rather, her laugh shows a human realism that can mistrust promises for the future which seem unreal and refuse forecasts of happiness which seem impossible. 'Her laughter is perhaps the only appropriate reaction to the promise. So she may convince herself and we may convince ourselves and have the denial contradicted: "No, you did laugh".'[14]

And yet while concentrating on Sarah's laughter we should not overlook the fact that there has already been mention of a laugh of Abraham's in the previous chapter, in Genesis 17. This laughter theologically opens up even wider perspectives. For it is worth noting one thing: when Sarah laughs, she does not yet know at whom she is laughing. So Sarah is not really laughing at God, but at men, guests in her husband's tent. In accordance with oriental custom, as a woman Sarah did not take part in the men's meal. She only heard what was said. And only when it dawns on her at whom she was laughing does she have a quite natural reaction: anxiety creeps into her heart and promptly leads her to dispute her own laughter. No one may laugh at God with impunity...

By contrast, the Abraham story is theologically more radical. For Abraham knew from the beginning whom he was dealing with. God had told Abraham his own name directly: El-Shaddai, the Almighty - and this (according to this source of the Pentateuch) had never happened to anyone since creation. Furthermore in the same appearance God had announced to Abraham what would in future be the foundation of a quite new relationship between him and humankind, the 'eternal covenant' (17.13) concluded between himself and Abraham's descendants. God had even held out the prospect of these descendants through Abraham's thus far barren wife. So here we find a key passage for the whole theology of the First Testament, indeed for the whole history of Israel: God's covenant promise to Abraham, which finds its visible expression in circumcision, the sign of the covenant (17.11-14).

And what does Abraham do when he hears that at the age of one hundred he will still be capable of fathering a child and at the age of ninety Sarah will still be capable of bearing it? Abraham falls down on his face – and laughs (17.17). So outwardly he performs the due gesture of humility to God, but he is laughing as he does so. This is not the laughter of joy, but quite clearly, in the light of the questions which Abraham now puts to God, it is similarly the laughter of unbelief. Abraham laughs at God, not like Sarah, silently and unsuspectingly, but audibly and directly. This is an unprecedented scene whose theological explosiveness traditional Old Testament exegesis has sought to play down. However, we must follow the Tübingen Old Testament scholar Walter Gross in interpreting it like this: 'The Abraham prostrate in worship before God and yet laughing at the same time is one of the most inscrutable images in Holy Scripture'[15] – inscrutable because here 'faith' manifestly presents itself in the garb of laughing doubt of God.

How inscrutable people must in fact have felt this picture to be can also be seen from the further tradition of the exegesis of this story about Abraham. What, for example, the Jew Paul has to say about Abraham in the first century can only be described (to quote Gross again) as 'violent reinterpretation'. In Paul, nothing is left of any doubt and unbelieving laughter in Abraham. As the apostle writes in his Letter to the Romans: 'He did not weaken in faith when he considered his own body, which was as good as dead because he was about a hundred years old, or when he considered the barrenness of Sarah's womb. No distrust made him waver concerning the promise of God, but he grew strong in his faith as he gave glory to God' (4.19f.). This is the precise opposite of what Genesis 17 in fact says: 'Then Abraham fell on his face and laughed.' At this decisive point there can be no question of a faith without weakness and without doubt, however strong Abraham's faith in God may have been later. On the contrary, the anthropological point of this story is that laughter expresses the doubting unbelief of human beings in the promises of God.

But the story about Abraham and Sarah also has a theological point. For it is indeed striking that in Abraham and Sarah we have people who can evidently laugh at God with impunity. Thus they both embody a theology of laughter in which human beings are also taken seriously in their unbelief in God. Even the mention of a rebuke from God in the Sarah story cannot disturb this picture, since this story too does not end in catastrophe, but has a happy ending. Human beings are not punished for their laughter, but are given by God what they declared to be impossible in their doubting laughter.

So the Sarah-Abraham story says this: God establishes himself and fulfils his purposes despite unbelieving human laughter. Had it been left to Abraham, Isaac the son whom Sarah would finally bring into the world would not have been born, and the people of Israel, which goes back to Isaac and then to Jacob, would not have existed at all. For initially Abraham was willing to be content with his son Ishmael, Ishmael who later was similarly to become the ancestor of a great people (17.20). But God sees himself as being above all this; he ignores the human unbelief expressed in laughter and renews his promise to Sarah that she will bear a child and the promise of the covenant to Isaac and his descendants (17.18f.). So after the birth of her son Isaac Sarah can say in overflowing happiness: 'God has made laughter for me; every one who hears will laugh over me' (21.6). Moreover it is no coincidence that her son is called Isaac, a literal translation of which is 'God laughs'. It means that in Isaac God laughs at human beings and their little faith. Isaac and thus Israel are (according to the original purpose of God) the gift of a God laughing in happiness at humankind.

So a shift can be recognized in this story of Abraham and Sarah: from sceptical laughter at God to the liberating laughter of everyone with God. The theological point of this story consists in the recognition that God allows even human laughter about God. It need not be suppressed or morally condemned – as in the history of Christian monasticism. Scripture itself does not exclude the comical, the laughable and doubt from the sphere of the holy. On the contrary, here is talk of a God who himself tolerates the laughing doubt of human beings and in the end turns it into the happy laughter of joy. The divine fulfilment of a possibility unexpected by human beings leads to the liberating laughter of human beings with their God.

3. God Laughs at the Rulers: Psalm 2

The story of Sarah spoke of anxiety, albeit an anxiety which is resolved happily in the end when all laugh with God. But not every story in the First Testament has this ending; quite the contrary.

Threatening laughter

If we bring in other texts, the perspective of God can become thoroughly frightening, threatening and dangerous. We have to turn to a second basic motif, which is expressed impressively in Psalm 2:

> Why do the nations conspire, and the people plot in vain?
>   The kings of the earth set themselves, and the rulers take
>   counsel together, against the Lord and his anointed, saying,
> 'Let us burst their bonds asunder, and cast their cords from
>   us.'
> He who sits in the heavens laughs; the Lord has them in
>   derision.
> Then he will speak to them in his wrath, and terrify them in
>   his fury, saying,
> 'I have set my king on Zion, my holy hill.'
> I will tell of the decree of the Lord; he said to me, 'You are my
>   son, today I have begotten you.
> Ask of me, and I will make the nations your heritage, and the
>   ends of the earth your possession.
> You shall break them with a rod of iron, and dash them in
>   pieces like a potter's vessel.
> Now therefore, O kings, be wise; be warned, O rulers of the
>   earth.'

Regardless of when this text may have been composed (before or after the exile) or whatever revisions it may have undergone; regardless of what functions it may have had (the expression of a pre-exilic royal ideology or the messianic hope of an oppressed post-exilic community; and regardless of whoever may have been the speaker (the real king of the past or only an expected messiah king[16]), in its final form as it has been included in the psalter it communicates the following experiences. The foreign peoples have rebelled, the nations have conspired against God the Lord and his 'anointed'. 'Anointed'? He is – we learn – the king appointed by God himself, who rules in 'Zion', i.e. in Jerusalem. In this psalm he is given unprecedented authority. For the king ruling in Jerusalem is understood as son of God. And as son this ruler also receives an inheritance, a possession: the peoples of the world, indeed the whole earth. So those who hear the psalm are meant to draw the conclusion that the real Lord to whom the world with all its nations and people belongs is Yahweh, the God of the elect people. To him history belongs; he is the real agent in history.

Now whether we read this text as a hymn of praise to the Israelite king on his accession to the throne, who as king of a small people is claiming tremendous authority over the world, or as the hope for an expected messiah king among an oppressed people, at the centre we have not so much this king himself as the powerful superiority of God. The symbol of this superiority is his throne in heaven, which is here deliberately set off against the kings on earth, who cannot even attack God's power when they band together. The theological point which this psalm seeks to make to those who use it is thus clear: no people, no nation on earth can shake the power of the God of Israel and his anointed; no ruler can establish a rule which goes against this God and his son. So Psalm 2 is a poem of threat and warning. It is an appeal to the great of the earth to desist from their plans and to subject themselves to the God of Israel and his representative (from now on or in the future), on pain of the wrath of God and destruction by his instrument, the king of 'Zion'.

The laughter of superiority

The most visible expression of this unassailable power of God is his laughter, a laughter of superiority and sovereignty, a knowing, mocking laughter from a God who sees through the situation on earth and can therefore only laugh mockingly at the vanity of human lust for domination. Hans-Joachim Kraus rightly notes in his commentary on the psalm: 'The king of Jerusalem knows Yahweh as the God over all the world, enthroned in heaven, who laughs at the plans of the rebels. Something of this laughter already resounds in verse 1, in the wondering question of the singer. The strident anthropomorphism bears witness to Yahweh the living God who reacts, who plays a passionate part in earthly affairs. Behind the king of Jerusalem there is not just any mythological power but the Lord who commands, who has everything in his hands and who "mocks" the deluded efforts of the rebels. This vision of the laughing and mocking heavenly Lord is a message of unprecedented prophetic weight.'[17]

If we compare this with the story of Abraham and Sarah, it is clear that here we have a radical change of perspective. Here the talk is no longer of human beings who laugh at God nor of a God who laughs happily with human beings. Here is talk of a God who laughs at people and nations and gets angry with them. The meaning is that God is amused at the plans of potentates to attack his rule in the form of his 'son', the king on Zion. With his laughter God shows the limits of such attempts. With his laughter God's mocking doubt on all human attempts to impose their domination against his will is revealed.

4. God Laughs at the Wicked: Problems with the Psalms

How far from harmless the picture of God is in this warning psalm (at any rate, God gives the Israelite king to understand that – if need be – he could 'shatter the nations with an iron rod'!) emerges from other psalms which are to some degree battle psalms. They are not directed abroad, against the rulers of the nations, but towards home, against the 'wicked'. And by wicked are meant those people who sin against God, despise his law and mock his commandments.

The sinner as mocker

The psalms of Israel in particular are full of massive polemic against such 'wicked' people, against the godless of every kind, i.e. people who act as if one need not take any notice of God and his commandments. The very first psalm of all in fact contrasts two archetypical figures: the wicked man and the just man:

> Blessed is the man who walks not in the counsel of the wicked,
> nor stands in the way of sinners, nor sits in the seat of scoffers;
> but his delight is in the law of the Lord, and on his law he
>   meditates day and night.
> He is like a tree planted by streams of water,
> that yields its fruit in its season, and its leaf does not wither.
> In all that he does, he prospers.
> The wicked are not so, but are like chaff which the wind drives
>   away.
> Therefore the wicked will not stand in the judgment, nor
>   sinners in the congregation of the righteous;
> for the Lord knows the way of the righteous, but the way of
>   the wicked will perish.

What is worth noting in this text, which opens the book of Psalms like a warning notice, is that here the wicked person is portrayed as a mocker, as one who laughs. The wicked man does not laugh in doubt about God like Abraham and Sarah, still less rejoicing with God, but in mockery against God. With him is contrasted true joy in God and God's commandments. Moreover this psalm expresses a remarkable assurance of salvation which draws on a certainty of God. And this assurance of salvation is all the more remarkable since it is coupled with an assurance that the wicked will come to judgment: the wicked man who laughs mockingly will not stand in the judgment, and will end in the abyss.

Here already we come across a dualism (wicked man, sinner, mocker on the one hand and the 'community of the righteous' on the other) which is characteristic of many psalms and at the same time problematical. Psalm 1 lays down once and for all a stereotype of the 'sinner' which since then has become engraved deeply on the souls of millions of people, and which has necessarily led to a hatred of all that is sinful. In particular *the identification of mockery and sin* is already made here; it was to have devastating consequences in the history of Christianity also, as if there could be no legitimate mockery in the interest of faith, as if the person who mocked was automatically alien to God.

Other psalms have even more vivid language here. Those who utter them not only mark off the community of the pious from the 'circle of mockers', but even claim God against the wicked. They evidently know that God is a God who himself laughs at the wicked and the mockers. Accordingly the theological strategy of such psalms is to overtrump the wicked and their mocking laughter with the opposite picture of a God with his mocking laughter. In this way the devil is to some degree to be driven out with Beelzebub. One example is Psalm 37, in which the singer almost automatically seems to know God's attitude to the wicked:

> The wicked plots against the righteous, and gnashes his teeth at him;
> but the Lord laughs at the wicked, for he sees that his day is coming.
> The wicked draw the sword and bend their bows,
> to bring down the poor and needy, to slay those who walk uprightly;
> their sword shall enter their own heart, and their bows shall be broken (37.12-15).

Psalm 59, in which God is also called on against the godless, is similar. Indeed in this psalm the singer does not even hesitate to call on God not to 'spare any of those who treacherously plot evil'. In other words, people call on their God to refuse grace to the wicked, not to give them a chance:

> Each evening they come back, howling like dogs and prowling about the city.
> There they are, bellowing with their mouths, and snarling with their lips – For 'Who,' they think, 'will hear us?'
> But you, Lord, laugh at them; you hold all the nations in derision (59.7-9).

The perspective shift from the story of Sarah and Abraham could hardly be greater. Here we are as far removed from a liberating laughter of human beings with God as from a laughter of scepticism and unbelief. Here we have a theology which has already developed a dualistic notion of redemption: humankind is divided into the community of the righteous and the circles of the wicked, mockers and sinners. In the light of this dualistic doctrine of redemption the image of God no longer seems reconciling, but divisive. The righteous make God their own supporter and are not afraid to appeal even to the limits of God's grace. Thus God is functionalized as the one who confirms their split picture of the world. In these circles the laughing God is the one who laughs at the other, whose annihilation is the desired aim. There is no longer anything about the laughter of God which brings reconciliation and makes peace; rather, it sets apart and divides. It becomes a weapon in the fight of the party of the just against the party of the wicked.

It is now already clear how enigmatic and ambivalent such laughter of God is. At any rate this divine laughter has nothing to do with joyful, happy laughter. It is also worlds removed from the laughter which Homer attributed to his gods. For as we saw, the 'Homeric laughter' of the gods is not aimed at the annihilation of the godless as is Yahweh's laughter in the Psalms. The laughter of the Olympian gods did not cause anxiety and bring death; it was not militant laughter against anyone in favour of a particular party, a particular people or ruler. The laughter of the Greek gods was above all directed at their like, and the character of their laughter was that of *Schadenfreude* or frivolity. It was an immoderate and heedless laughter beyond all human reason and human ethic, a laughter 'beyond good and evil'.

So it is no coincidence that Friderich Nietzsche devoted a section to the 'Olympian blasphemers' in his work *Beyond Good and Evil*: 'Despite the philosopher who, as a genuine Englishman, tried to bring laughter into bad repute in all thinking minds – "Laughing is a bad infirmity of human nature, which every thinking mind would strive to overcome" (Hobbes) – I would even allow myself to rank philosophers according to the quality of their laughing – up to those who are capable of *golden* laughter. And supposing that gods also philosophize, which I am strongly inclined to believe, owing to many reasons – I have no doubt that they also know how to laugh in a superman-like and new fashion – And at the expense of all serious things! Gods are fond of ridicule; it seems that they cannot refrain from laughter even in holy matters.'[18]

The laughter of God in certain psalms of the First Testament is quite different. Their singers do not understand the smallest joke.

Their God certainly likes mockery, but hardly in the sense 'beyond good and evil', beyond holy and unholy, mentioned by Niezsche. It is inconceivable that the God of these psalms could not 'refrain from laughter even in holy matters'! For the God of these psalm singers is the guarantor of good against evil, of the holy against the unholy. His laughter is the divisive laughter of a partisan God whom the pious would like best to see denying free grace to all the impious...

5. The Inscrutable Laughter of God

So there is no longer anything liberating about the laughter of God which the singers of certain psalms conjure up. Rather, it has become coupled with mockery, which can extend as far as the frontier with sarcasm. Just as in the Abraham story the image of the human being threatens to become ambiguous, indeed uncanny, so too does the image of God here. And indeed there are dimensions of the image of God in the Hebrew Bible where this ambiguity and uncanny nature of God are emphasized by his laugh: an impenetrable, enigmatic laugh.

Laughter as a reward at the end

The book of Job is one example. This book talks of laughter in a twofold sense, i.e. of two modes of laughter which could not be more opposite. One mode is that of offering comfort for the future: laughter as eschatological, ultimate reality. This is the way of Job's friends. For already in the fifth chapter one of the friends, Eliphaz, attempts to comfort Job by saying: 'Behold, happy is the man whom God reproves; therefore do not despise the chastening of the Almighty' (5.17). By that this 'friend' means that it is precisely the afflicted who is the friend of God. Why? Because according to all experiences one day God will reward the one who is chastized. Thus to some degree the nearness of God to the sufferer is already 'guaranteed'. The sufferer will laugh again:

For he (God) wounds, but he binds up;
he smites, but his hands heal.
He will deliver you from six troubles;

in seven there shall no evil touch you.
In famine he will redeem you from death,
and in war from the power of the sword.
You shall be hid from the scourge of the tongue,
and shall not fear destruction when it comes.
At destruction and famine you shall laugh,
and shall not fear the beasts of the earth (5.18-22).

Another friend, Bildad of Shuah, expresses a similar notion:

He will fill your mouth with laughter,
your mouth and your lips with shouting.

The rhetoric of consolation – for thousands a variation in the
history of religions: laughter as the reward for the tormented, as
hope for the future, as consolation in all despair. The psalms also
know this motif:

When the Lord restored the fortunes of Zion,
we were like those who dream.
Then our mouth was filled with laughter,
and our tongue with shouts of joy;
then they said among the nations,
'The Lord has done great things for them.'
The Lord has done great things for us;
we are glad.
Restore our fortunes, O Lord,
like the watercourses in the Negeb!
May those who sow in tears
reap with shouts of joy.
He that goes forth weeping,
 bearing the seed for sowing,
shall come home with shouts of joy,
bringing his sheaves with him (Ps.126).

God laughs at the guiltless: Job's experience

Comfort in all despair: all this does not correspond to Job's
experiences. The rhetoric of reward will not sort out his cause
with God. He rejects all the well-meaning attempts of his friends
in this direction. Why? Because God – in Job's view – has entangled

60

himself far too much in self-contradictions, has become dark and enigmatic. Job's experience is that God can manifestly torment human beings without having any obvious occasion for doing so, that God can punish men and women with suffering although these have hitherto – like Job – lived a 'blameless and upright life' before God. So what kind of God is it who so deprives the innocent of their happiness? Does that not make the Almighty an arbitrary God before whom human beings have no chance, because in any case they cannot compete with the greatness of God?

> How then can I answer him, choosing my words with him?
> Though I am innocent, I cannot answer him; I must appeal
>   for mercy to my accuser.
> If I summoned him and he answered me, I would not believe
>   that he was listening to my voice (9.14-16).

So that is the experience of Job: God does not hear! God is not on the side of justice. On the contrary, even the righteous does not escape. 'Without reason' God multiplies his 'wounds', does not let him get his breath, fills him 'with bitterness' (9.17f.). Certainly Job himself feels utterly 'guiltless' (9.21). But what use is this guiltlessness to him before such a God, who evidently punishes guilty and innocent to the same degree?

> I am blameless; I regard not myself; I loathe my life.
> It is all one; therefore I say, he destroys both the blameless and
>   the wicked.
> When disaster brings sudden death, he mocks at the calamity
>   of the innocent (9.21-23).

God laughs at the anxiety of the innocent! With this experience of God of the man from Uz, described in chapter 9 of the book of Job, one of the boldest chapters of Old Testament theology, the image of God in the Hebrew Bible becomes completely uncanny. For in Job we have someone who has neither exalted himself against God as a ruler nor sinned against God as a wicked man, but rather has all his life feared God and avoided evil (1.8). With Job we are confronted with someone who is conscious of no guilt and who yet one day felt God's scourges on his body, scourges which he has to interpret as an expression of God's laughter at his own anguish, the anguish of the innocent. God seems to be playing a joke, further to torment the innocent in his anguish.

There is no doubt about it: in such a laugh all trust in God threatens to be lost; God becomes enigmatically unscrutable, arbitrarily uncanny.

No wonder, too, that the final theological redactors of the book of Job did everything possible to cope theologically with this experience of God in chapter 9. Indeed – to exaggerate somewhat – one can say that the overall theological tendency of the book of Job is one single attempt to refute this experience of God. The whole of the book of Job seems to have been written against chapter 9. For in the final form as we now have it, 'Job' has as its theological point that in the end God is not the enigmatic arbitrary God that he first seemed to be to Job. Towards the end there is the twofold insight:

1. Certainly, human beings often cannot perceive the structure of meaning and order in creation – there Job is right. So, 'The Almighty – we cannot find him' (37.23). But at the same time it is true that:

2. This insight is no reason to infer that there is a total lack of meaning and order in the world or that God is purely arbitrary. God is no cynical player 'in heaven' who even enjoys the anguish of innocent human beings. God does not sin against human beings. Despite everything he is 'great in power and justice, and abundant righteousness he will not violate' (37.23).[19]

So quite deliberately at the end of the book of Job we do not have the believer laughed at by God but the man who has been put right by God. Thus the basic tendency of Job aims at restoring the relationship of trust between God and man which has been destroyed by inscrutable experiences – despite all the other questions that human beings may still have. But since people have read the book of Job critically, they have doubted this theological way out taken by the final redactors of this book. For many people the experience of God of chapter 9 may have been relativized, but it has not been refuted.[20]

Laughter as sin: biblical Wisdom

Whatever may have had to be said about the phenomenon of laughter in the First Testament so far, in the texts we have seen we have not found so much a devaluation, even a disparagement of laughter as a textual tradition which shows the not unproblematical identification of mockery and sin. Only in the late documents of the First Testament, in the writings of the so-called Wisdom literature, in Ecclesiastes, Jesus Sirach, Proverbs and Wisdom, do we find what the old blind monk in Eco's novel fanatically attempted to practise: an explicit denunciation of human laughter. Moreover – as we saw – mediaeval monasticism above all referred to passages from these writings when it wanted to demonstrate the 'worthlessness' of laughter.

What is said here in the Wisdom literature about laughter far exceeds the basically pessimistic attitude of Koheleth, for whom both weeping and laughter have their 'time' (3.4), and who out of sheer world-weariness and pessimism sinks to the statement, 'I said of laughter, "It is mad"' (2.2; cf. also Proverbs 14.13). Rather, in the educational and admonitory writings from the wisdom schools of ancient Palestine the deterrent picture of the fool is quite specifically contrasted with the ideal picture of the wise man. But what characterizes the fool? Among other things the fact that he laughs. His laughter is the sign of his frivolity and lack of thought:

> The mind of a fool is like a broken jar; it will hold no
>   knowledge.
> When a man of understanding hears a wise saying, he will
>   praise it and add to it;
> when a reveller hears it he laughs at it, and casts it behind his
>   back (Sirach 21.14f.).

Furthermore, for the wisdom teachers of Palestine the laughter of the fool is not just the expression of his frivolity and lack of thought, but also an expression of his sinful pleasure:

> Among stupid people watch for a chance to leave, but among
>   thoughtful people stay on.
> The talk of fools is offensive, and their laughter is wantonly
>   sinful (Sirach 27.12f.).

No, there is no longer talk here of people like Abraham and Sarah who could laugh at God without God feeling himself sinfully challenged. On the contrary, the motif of God's laughter at the wicked, which we have already seen in the Psalms, is particularly dominant in the Wisdom literature. Here too it is God himself who laughs at the wicked and thus gives them over to complete annihilation. Here, too, God's laughter is ultimately a violent laughter of annihilation. The wicked should to some degree keep their laughter in check, drowned by the laughter of God who hurls them into the abyss.

> The wicked see the end of the wise man,
>> and will not understand what the Lord purposed for him,
>> and for what he kept him safe.
> They will see, and will have contempt for him,
>> but the Lord will laugh them to scorn.
> After this they will become dishonoured corpses,
>> and an outrage among the dead for ever;
> because he will dash them speechless to the ground,
>> and shake them from the foundations;
> they will be left utterly dry and barren, and they will suffer anguish,
>> and the memory of them will perish (Wisdom 4.17-19).

In short, in the First Testament we have a wide palette of ambiguous laughter – human laughter and God's laughter.

For human beings:
• there is the sceptical unbelieving laughter of men and women at God, which can change into a liberating, joyful laughter with God;
• and there is the unconcerned, indeed sinful laughter of the fool, which will be silenced, since the seriousness of the wise is contrasted with the laughing fool.

As far as God is concerned:
• There is the joyful, liberating laughter of God with the doubters and sceptics;
• there is the superior, mocking laughter of God who demonstrates the limits of the non-Israelite rulers and all wicked men and sinners, and in this way divides and sets a limit;
• and there is the uncanny, enigmatic, inscrutable laughter of God at innocent people which is destructive of trust in its manifest arbitrariness.

III

The Laughter of Christians: New Testament Foundations

1. The Laughter of the Gnostic

Our next question is: which of all these motifs have found their way into the Second Testament? Wasn't John Chrysostom right in observing that Christ never laughed?

Christ laughs at Jesus on the cross

But what about the following scene? In the week before Easter, Peter in the Temple at Jerusalem is told by Jesus what he needs to know about the suffering and death of the Master. He is to understand, and thus learn better to cope with the death of Christ. The right insight will communicate strength and comfort. Here Christ laments the error and blindness to which human beings have succumbed and conjures up the need for true knowledge. And suddenly Peter sees in a vision the scene of the imprisonment and crucifixion of Jesus and asks:

'What is this that I see, O Lord? Is it you alone whom they take, and do you lay hold of me? Or who is this who is glad beside you and laughs? And another they strike upon his feet and on his hands?'
The Saviour said to me:
'He whom you see beside the tree glad and laughing, this is the living Jesus. But he into whose hands and feet they drive the nails is his fleshly (likeness), the "ransom", which (alone) they (are able to) put to shame. That came into being after his likeness. But look on him and on me!' But when I had looked, I said:
'Lord, no one sees you, let us flee from here!'
But he said to me:

65

'I have told you that they (are) blind. But you, see how little they know what they say.'[1]

What a scene! The living Christ, the risen saviour, stands beside the cross intended for him and watches while another man is nailed to the wood in his place. He laughs, and his laughter is evidently all the more justified since the executioners do not know that the true Christ has long since parted from his earthly body and they are now nailing only a physical likeness to the cross: a pseudo-Jesus. The executioners are among those who are unsuspecting, ignorant. The redeemer alone embodies true knowledge. And true knowledge is denoted by a Greek word: gnosis!

The names and settings of the scene depicted above sound as though they have been taken from the New Testament, but at the same time the scene is miles from the New Testament. A Christ who after his transportation to heaven can look on laughing while someone else is nailed bloodily to the cross? A Christ who is gently amused at the blindness and folly of human beings, and could stage a cheap deception? This is inconceivable for the New Testament. Moreover such a text presupposes a particular image of God and the saviour, that of Gnosticism, a religious movement from late antiquity, which was to become the great spiritual rivalry to early Christianity from the second century on.[2] Moreover the scene which is depicted comes from an Apocalypse of Peter which may have been composed in Gnostic circles at the end of the second or beginning of the third century CE. As a result of the discovery of a Gnostic library in the city of Nag Hammadi in Middle Egypt we have meanwhile acquired information about Gnosticism at first hand and not, as previously, at second hand (through quotations from the anti-Gnostic writings of the church fathers).

The laughing saviour

But the church fathers had already given a precise report that the Gnostics had a particular image of Christ – thus e.g. Irenaeus of Lyons, the fighter against heresies. And this image was completely dominated by Christ the saviour, a heavenly figure who had been sent down to earth by God. It was quite incompatible with the divinity of this saviour that he should die an utterly human death. Before that this Christ had to be transported from the earth into heavenly glory: a substitute had to suffer the shameful death in his place. Irenaeus had already summarized the Gnostic doctrine of the impassibility of the saviour like this:

> But the father without birth and without name, perceiving that they would be destroyed, sent his own first-begotten *nous* (he it is who is called Christ) to bestow deliverance on them that believe in him, from the power of those who made the world. He appeared, then, on earth as a man, to the notions of these powers, and wrought miracles. Wherefore he himself did not suffer death, but Simon, a certain man of Cyrene, being compelled, bore the cross in his stead; so that this latter being transfigured by him, that he might be thought to be Jesus, was crucified, through ignorance and error, while Jesus himself received the form of Simon and standing by laughed at them.[3]

Here Irenaeus had in fact made a point which was decisive for numerous Christian Gnostics: Christ cannot have experienced being human with all its consequences, otherwise he would not be the divine saviour. Texts from the Nag Hammadi library confirm this notion, in which the figure of Simon of Cyrene plays the decisive substitute role. Thus in 'The Second Treatise of the Great Seth', Christ is made to say:

> For my death, which they think happened, (happened) to them in their error and blindness, since they nailed their man unto their death. For their insight (Ennoias) did not see me, for they were deaf and blind. But in doing these things they condemn themselves. Yes, they saw me; they punished me. It was another, their father, who drank the gall and the vinegar; it was not I. They struck me with the reed; it was another, Simon, who bore the cross on his shoulder. It was another upon whom they placed the crown of thorns. But I was rejoicing in the height... and I was laughing at their ignorance.[4]

So Gnosticism knows the laughing saviour,[5] in complete contrast to the New Testament. Here we have a paradoxical shift of fronts. For the laughter of the Gnostic saviour contains the possibility in principle of humanizing the saviour. But it is striking that his laughter does not make the Gnostic saviour more human. Despite his laughter he remains the superior heavenly being, the one who is divinely exalted, who may not exhaust the full depth of humanity (including suffering). Moreover the laughter of the Gnostic saviour is strictly speaking not human laughter but the laughter of one who is exalted, a heavenly being, a laughter of divine superiority and mockery which is in the line of tradition that we know from Psalms 2 and 59. The laughter of the Gnostic saviour is comparable to the laughter of God who mocks his enemies. So the saviour's laughter does not humanize him but intensifies his 'docetic' character, which prevents the saviour as a human being from really sharing all the consequences of humanity.

Here the Jesus Christ of the New Testament is quite different. And the question now arises formally: what about the historical Jesus himself? Unlike the Gnostics, the New Testament authors leave no doubt that Jesus of Nazareth was human in the full sense of the word. *Vere homo*! Yet the one thing Jesus is not portrayed as having done in the New Testament is having laughed. At least statistically, John Chrysostom was right! What then? We would do well first to turn to the figure of the historical Jesus and then move forward from belief in Jesus as the Christ (as proclaimed by Paul) to the theological foundation of a Christian theology of laughter.

2. New Creation – New Time

No lengthy explanation is needed. From all that we can infer from the Gospels, while the statement that 'Christ never laughed' is statistically correct, to draw any further theological conclusion from this is as wayward and false an interpretation of the figure of the historical Jesus as the other statement about a Jesus who looks on laughing while another man is crucified in his place.

We need not engage in any exegetical gymnastics here and pedantically attempt to demonstrate that Jesus himself made jokes, that some of his remarks were 'witty', that Jesus too had a sense of irony and humour. Often enough that sounds like narrow Christian apologetic and theological jumping on the bandwaggon with the slogan 'Our Jesus too!' Here people have all too often read something into the text and then got it out again – to the perplexity of a bewildered readership.[6] And what does it mean for someone with much exegetical acuteness to have discovered the playful character of some sayings of Jesus and the comic element in some of his miracles: the herd of swine is bewitched, the cripple runs around again, water changes into wine which is even better than the previous supply? However, the reverse is just as unsatisfying. For in that case – using a 'hermeneutics of suspicion', one would have to suppose that the Gospels deliberately suppressed, tendentiously deleted any laughter of Jesus out of a prejudice against laughter, for moral or political reasons. But there is no evidence of that anywhere.

Giving birth and laughing

I think that we get further if we look at the figure of Jesus of Nazareth as a whole, at the profile of his message, at the distinctive character of his behaviour. We must already attempt to understand him in terms of his mysterious, ultimately unfathomable 'nature', in order to be able to find responsible answers to our questions. And the essential thing seems to me to be this. While in the New Testament we do not have the picture of a 'laughing saviour' in the Gnostic sense, far less do we have a Jesus who denounced laughter and joy. Rather, through the Gospels there runs the warm current of a joy at creation and human beings which emanates from Jesus.

The birth stories, especially those of Luke, make a clear statement here. More than any other evangelist, Luke not only attaches supreme importance to the fact that with the appearance of Jesus a messianic age has dawned, but strikingly interprets this age as a time of joy. And a time of joy without laughter is not worth the name. It is striking that already in the first two chapters of his Gospel the term 'joy' occurs as a characteristic of the new beginning. For already Elizabeth, the mother of John the Baptist, the forerunner of Jesus, is told by an angel: 'And you will have joy and gladness, and many will rejoice at his birth' (1.14). And not content with that, when Elisabeth meets the mother of Jesus, she feels her child move: 'When the voice of your greeting came to my ears, the babe in my womb leaped for joy' (1.44). This is the anticipatory joy of the forerunner.

This joy which has dawned in the figure of the forerunner of course becomes intensified with the birth of the Messiah himself. So Luke puts a song of joy on Mary's lips immediately after her encounter with Elizabeth – utterly symbolic in its warmth and exuberance: 'My soul magnifies the Lord, and my spirit rejoices in God my Saviour, for he has regarded the low estate of his handmaiden. For behold, henceforth all generations will call me blessed' (1.46-48). In the apocryphal Infancy Gospel of James this theme is further intensified; here Mary, still pregnant, is depicted as a weeping yet also laughing mother. With an allusion to the polarization which will come about with the appearance of the Messiah among the nations (cf. Genesis 25.23; Luke 2.34), this Gospel reports of Joseph and Mary:

> And Joseph turned round and saw her sad, and said within himself: 'Perhaps that which is within her is paining her.' And Joseph turned around and saw her laughing. And he said to her: 'Mary, why is it that I see your face at one time laughing and at another sad?' And she said to him: 'Joseph, I see with my eyes two peoples, one weeping and lamenting and one rejoicing and exalting.'
>
> And they came half the way, and Mary said to him: 'Joseph, take me down from the ass, for the child within me presses me to come forth.'[7]

Messianic jubilation – messianic joy; that is also what is spoken of in the Gospel of Luke. Here the evangelist describes the birth of the new redeemer not only as a private event but above all as a cosmic event: angels suddenly appear in Bethlehem and proclaim 'great joy' to the shepherds. The latter are not to keep their joy to themselves but to communicate it to the 'whole people' (2.10). And what is meant by this joy if not the messianic time that has dawned with Jesus, a time of the 'kingdom of God' which breaks into the world of traditional piety and religion as a counter-reality?

Laughter for pleasure in life: a theme of myth

Here Luke – whether consciously or unconsciously – has produced a variation on a theme of myth and poetry. For in myth and poetry the time of renewal, of fertility, of birth and rebirth, is at the same time a time of laughter. Thus in the famous Fourth Eclogue of the Roman poet Virgil (70-19 BCE), a century before Luke, there is mention of a child of God whose birth similarly ushers in a new

70

age. This newborn child laughs, and in so doing betrays 'his supernatural descent: he is from the family of Helios, the smiling god (of the sun)'.[8] This terminology has lasted down to the present day, when we talk of the 'smiling sun'. It refers to a mythical origin and associates with the sun new life, new creation, new time.

Laughter and new life: we again know this connection from the apocryphal writings of early Christianity. These not only tell of a laughing mother but also say of the newborn Jesus that he did not cry like other children, but 'laughed', and 'smiled with the most sweet smile'.[9] This is a thought which then found its way into one of the most famous of Christmas carols:

> Silent night, holy night,
> Son of God, O how bright
> Love is smiling from Thy face!
> Strikes for us now the hour of grace,
> Saviour, since Thou art born!

Laughter and giving birth: we also know this connection from Zoroaster, the founder of the Persian religion, who is reported as being the only person to have laughed on the day of his birth. For the sun stands at the centre of the Zoroastrian cult and here too means the end of darkness, new beginning. We also know the association from Greek-Egyptian sources, where a treatise on creation says: 'God laughed seven times, and at his laughter the seven gods who embrace the world were born... The seventh time he laughed with tears of joy, and Psyche was born.'[10] Also from Egypt comes a great hymn to the Nile which speaks of laughter, when after times of utter deprivation and hunger the inundation of the Nile again appears at the right level: 'When the Nile rises, then the land rejoices, then everyone is joyful. Every jaw opens in laughter, every tooth is bared.'[11]

There are also parallels to this in fairy tales and folksongs: laughter as an expression of fertility, of the fullness of life, of resistance against death. The Tübingen German scholar Walter Haug has drawn attention to this. He sums up the evidence like this: 'In the fairy tale the sad princess must be made to laugh if she is to be won, i.e. if the wedding is to take place. There are parallels in myth; the rain god must be made to laugh so that he lets fall his water: laughter and rain, i.e. fertility, belong together.

That is also the significance of ritual laughter in the Eastern cultic drama. There is a bringer of salvation at whose laughter the earth begins to blossom, or the roses laugh, and so on. Laughter from the fullness of life can at the same time be understood as laughter against all that is contrary to life. For example, there are folk songs from Serbia in which the mother restores her dead son to life by laughing; or the father kills his child on divine orders and Jesus comes and laughs with all his might, so that it revives. Or there are customs: parents laugh when a child dies to protect their other children from death.'[12]

3. The Warm Current of Jesus' Joy

The warm current of messianic joy persists through Jesus' life as he begins to speak in public and to perform his signs. Here, too, Luke may have understood Jesus correctly when – again in a completely symbolic way – at the beginning of his public ministry he puts on his lips a saying from the prophet Isaiah. The scene is the synagogue in Jesus' home town of Nazareth:

> The Spirit of the Lord is upon me,
> because he has anointed me
> to preach good news to the poor.
> He has sent me
> to proclaim release to the captives
> and recovering of sight to the blind,
> to set at liberty those who are oppressed,
> to proclaim the acceptable year of the Lord (4.18f.).

Messianic jubilation

The point of this symbolic scene should be evident to anyone who knows scripture: in Jesus' person the prophet Isaiah's vision of 'God's anointed' is conjured up here yet again. With the appearance of this anointed one the Lord's 'year of grace' dawns, and all who knew their Isaiah were aware that this saying of Isaiah continues:

> He has sent me...

to comfort all who mourn,
to grant to those who mourn in Zion –
to give them a garland instead of ashes,
the oil of gladness instead of mourning,
the mantle of praise instead of a faint spirit (61.2f.).

So it is joy and praise that accompany Jesus's appearance. Messianic enthusiasm breaks out. This comes to a climax at the entry of Jesus into Jerusalem, which Luke conceives as a reprise of the message of the angels to the shepherds of Bethlehem, now depicted as having been 'fulfilled': 'As he was now drawing near, at the descent of the Mount of Olives, the whole multitude of the disciples began to rejoice and praise God with a loud voice for all the mighty works that they had seen, saying, "Blessed is the King who comes in the name of the Lord! Peace in heaven and glory in the highest"' (19.37f.).

Granted, this same Luke puts on the lips of Jesus in his 'Sermon in the Plain' a warning against laughter which has the stamp of the Wisdom literature: 'Woe to you that laugh now, for you shall mourn and weep' (6.25). And why shouldn't this statement be authentic? Why shouldn't Jesus have criticized superficial laughter, which deceived itself over the endangering of life? But it is wrong to conclude from this that Jesus was deadly serious, with no sense of humour, as church fathers and monks did. For the same Jesus holds out the prospect of laughter for all those who weep: 'Blessed are you who weep now, for you shall laugh' (6.21). And there is no reason for postponing this laughter purely to the Last Day, if one has properly understood Jesus and his basic attitude to life.

On the contrary, a force evidently emanated from Jesus of Nazareth which was capable of changing people's hearts and ridding them of anxiety (Luke 19.37; 24.41). Again the apocryphal works have fewer inhibitions about speaking of Jesus as one who laughs. For example, in the Infancy Gospel of Thomas it is reported that as a boy Jesus already got the better of an old teacher called Zacchaeus to such a degree that he was ultimately driven to despair. We then read:

And while the Jews were trying to console Zacchaeus, the child laughed aloud and said: 'Now let that which is yours bear fruit, and let the blind in heart see. I have come from above to curse

73

them and call them to the thing above, as he commanded who sent me for your sakes.' And when the boy had finished speaking, immediately all who had fallen under his curse were healed.[13]

All this means that Jesus' ministry, Jesus' message, Jesus' activity and laughter belong together. His was a laughter of joy, a laughter of healing, a laughter of the transformation of hearts, a laughter against cosmic and psychological darkness. So any denuncation of laughter which refers to an alleged model of Christ is absurd. Could laughter have been alien to the one who went around with his followers through the land, had innumerable meals with them, included sinners and outcasts in these meals, took part in festivals and parties? Could the one of whom his opponents asserted that he was a 'glutton and winebibber', a 'friend of tax collectors and sinners' (Luke 7.34), have made laughter tabu? That is inconceivable. What is more characteristic of Jesus is his vivid talk about the kingdom of God, using imagery like marriage and feasting, and an awareness that with his own appearance this kingdom had dawned once and for all. All those who are disciples of Christ can feel that they are guests at a wedding: 'The Pharisees and the scribes said to him, "The disciples of John fast often and offer prayers, and so do the disciples of the Pharisees, but yours eat and drink." And Jesus said to them, "Can you make wedding guests fast while the bridegroom is with them?"' (Luke 5.33).

God's special joy over sinners

Now the deepest reason for Jesus' joy may have been his experience of God. For the God of whom Jesus tells in his parables is no God with an ambiguous laugh, nor a God whose laughter at rulers, wicked or even innocent people would be mocking and uncanny. He is not a God whose laughter divides, separates and condemns. On the contrary, Jesus' image of God strikingly dispenses with these inscrutable or polarizing features. Rather, Jesus' delight in human beings (and particularly children) is grounded:
• in his own delight in God which the evangelist Luke reports when he makes Jesus exclaim in a moment of enthusiastic exal-

tation, 'rejoicing', 'I thank you, Father, Lord of heaven and earth' (10.2);

• in the joy of God himself, particularly over sinners, the lost, and those who have incurred guilt. According to the parable of the lost sheep there is more 'joy' in heaven over the one sinner who repents than over ninety-nine just persons who need no repentance (Luke 15.7). The parable of the last coin (Luke 15.8-10) carries the same message. And according to the parable of the prodigal son, God is like a father who after the unexpected return of his son begins to celebrate a 'joyful feast' (Luke 15.24). No, the God of Jesus is not a God who laughs at human beings, mocks the wicked, and writes off sinners. Instead of any ambiguous laughter of God the New Testament knows God's joy, a joy which must necessarily express itself in laughter, but one to which laughter is not alien. It is therefore no chance that the basic formula for Jesus's cause is *euangelion*, good news, and not *dysangelion*, threatening news.

Here we get a small glimpse of that mystery which still surrounds Jesus of Nazareth, the mystery of his inner freedom which is closely bound up with his experience of God and makes him capable in individual instances of putting himself above religious tabus, social conventions and traditional rituals. This inner freedom of his from all compulsion, narrowness, legalism in religion (not to be confused with a sweeping antinomianism, even an opposition to the Torah) has a parallel in what Jesus called the 'kingdom of God': a reality which functions by other laws and is structured by other criteria than those allowed by the traditional religious system. It was a reality which freed him to live in the world without selling himself to it, to be in the world and yet have his focal point elsewhere.

So Jesus has a specific form of freedom from care which contrasts so completely with any anxiety of mind and craving for assurance of the kind to which we have become accustomed:

Therefore I tell you, do not be anxious about your life, what you shall eat or what you shall drink, nor about your body, what you shall put on. Is not life more than food, and the body more than clothing? Look at the birds of the air; they neither sow nor reap nor gather into barns, and yet your heavenly Father feeds them. Are you not of more value than they (Matthew 6.25f.).

In his *Critique of Cynical Reason* (1983), the philosopher Peter Sloterdijk drew attention to an illuminating parallel between the Greek cynic Diogenes of Sinope and Jesus of Nazareth. For the Greeks, Diogenes, the man who lived in a barrel by choice, embodied the ideal of inner freedom and joyful relaxation with extreme contentment. Hence the famous story of when the great ruler Alexander the Great visited Diogenes in his barrel and granted him a wish. Diogenes' reply is also famous: 'Get out of my light!' Sloterdijk rightly concludes: 'Alexander, who pursued his hunger for power to the frontiers of India, found his match in an outwardly inconspicuous, indeed run-down philosopher. In reality life is not for the activists or for those with cautious minds. Here the anecdote about Alexander has points of contact with Jesus' parable about the birds of the air who do not sow and reap and yet live as the freest creatures under God's heaven. Diogenes and Jesus are united in their irony against work in society which goes beyond what is necessary and merely serves to extend power. What the birds taught to Jesus was taught to Diogenes by a mouse, who became his model of contentment.'[14] Indeed if there is 'irony' of Jesus anywhere in the New Testament, it is here: in the chapters of the Sermon on the Mount which have been handed down to us by the evangelist Matthew (5-7); in irony about religious show (praying and fasting), about the mentality of accumulating things (laying up treasure), against petty worries and hypocrisy.

However, unlike Diogenes Jesus did not retreat from the world. On the contrary, Jesus claimed God for his lack of concern in a way which became an intolerable provocation to the pious, above all to the pious in power. Jesus' joy in God was therefore anything but private clowning or self-ironical harmlessness. It had consequences. For evidently the religious power cartel (the priestly caste and the scribes) could not cope with a God who took more delight 'over one sinner who repents than over ninety-nine just men who need no repentance' (Luke 15.7), and who like the father of the prodigal son rewards the repentant rebel more generously than the good and the true.

Here we may have Jesus' retort to the images of God in the psalms quoted earlier. The God who emerges, say, in the parables of Luke is not a God who laughs at sinners, but one who embraces them; he does not cause anxiety to the guilty or even the guiltless, but raises them up. Moreover Jesus' dealings with sinners have none of the threatening gestures of particular psalmists. On the contrary, Jesus felt himself sent in particular to the lost of the house of Israel...

So it is no coincidence that the joy of Jesus, which is deeply rooted in God's joy in all his creatures, must inevitably prove to be critical of power, break tabus, and liberate in a scandalous way. If we read the stories about Jesus from this aspect, we can note their peculiarities. The provocative joy, the kingdom of God theology which extends frontiers and breaks tabus, manifests itself in the way in which Jesus uses grotesque imagery ('It is easier for a camel to go through the eye of a needle than for a rich man to enter the kingdom of God', Mark 10.25), in the use of bold parables (all the parables about the 'lost' which Luke has brought together in Chapter 15), in the use of disarming answers ('Let him among you without sin cast the first stone', John 8.7), and the use of radical paradoxes ('Let the dead bury their dead', Luke 9.60), or in perplexing beatitudes:[15]

> Blessed are you poor,
> for yours is the kingdom of God.
> Blessed are you that hunger now,
> for you shall be satisfied.
> Blessed are you that weep now,
> for you shall laugh.
> Blessed are you when men hate you,
> and when they exclude you and revile you,
> and cast out your name as evil,
> on account of the Son of man!
> Rejoice in that day and leap for joy,
> for behold your reward is great in heaven (Luke 6.20-23).[16]

The picture of the laughing Jesus

So it is anything but artistic exaggeration or a theological misinterpretation for a laughing Jesus to be depicted in pictures or on posters. The Austrian writer Alois Brandstetter has described an encounter with such a picture of Jesus and has rightly focussed his experiences like this:

Around the middle of the 1960s, in a room in a Protestant student hostel in Saarbrücken, I saw alongside the then customary posters of Ché Guevara and Karl Marx an unusual picture of Christ, a laughing Christ with a face wrinkled in laughter and showing his teeth. The picture had the effect on me that had been intended by the painter and those who had bought it and hung it: it gave me a shock. This was because the expression of the laughing Christ was so different from the earnestness of traditional depictions of Christ, the depictions of the suffering and crucified Jesus, the *Ecce homo* pictures, the man of grief, and also the Sacred Heart pictures. One has only to look at the period between baroque and the Nazarenes to see how Jesus almost always, or at least very often, bears the marks of the wounds as a presupposition of his imminent suffering or as a recollection of the suffering that the risen Christ has undergone. The laughing Jesus was evidently meant by the painter as a Jesus who was laughing at someone. The young people in the hostel, some of whom were studying theology, explained to me that he was laughing at the men of the *church*, at the *men* of the church (that is the way in which the women in particular saw it). Since he had not been taken seriously by the theologians, above all by the controversial theologians, because they had not wanted to understand him and as it were had doubly made him a butt for their own thoughts, he was now laughing mockingly at them. Being ecumenical (or what they understood by that), the young people did not want to understand their Jesus as a Protestant Jesus in the sense that he took the side of Protestant theology and laughed at the Catholics and Baptists, but as Protestant in a 'fundamental', radical, to some degree free religious, unconfessional sense. So Christ is *played off* against the church or the churches, in a direct, meaningful way.[17]

Even if one has theological and exegetical reservations about simply playing off Jesus against the church like this, this picture of the laughing Christ makes an essential point. Here is neither laughter at God nor laughter at the wicked nor laughter at unsuspecting and blinded people. All that is alien to Jesus. Jesus' laughter is the expression of a freedom for God which bursts bounds and breaks tabus.

However, the reason why Jesus did not laugh *at* God does not lie in the fact that, unlike Abraham and Sarah, he had no cause for doing so. The reason lies elsewhere. Unlike Abraham, Jesus did not receive 'impossible' promises of God but embodied them himself. He himself in person was God's impossible concern – particularly for those who were despised and marginalized in the name of God. Jesus evidently ventured quite directly to claim God's authority for his words and symbolic actions and to act in the name of God at points where some of his contemporaries could least accept this. Here, moreover, lies the root of his fatal conflict.

4. The Laughed-at Jesus

As we saw, the New Testament authors do not report that Jesus ever laughed, though this should not lead us to draw false conclusions. But they often report something else: Jesus was laughed at. He was evidently one of those people who drew the laughter of others upon himself. And this evidently already happened during his lifetime.

The foolishness of God in person

Let's take as an example the story of the daughter of Jairus, the leader of the synagogue, which is told by Mark:

> While Jesus was still speaking, there came from the ruler's house some who said, 'Your daughter is dead. Why trouble the Teacher any further?' But ignoring what they said, Jesus said to the ruler of the synagogue, 'Do not fear, only believe', and he allowed no one to follow him except Peter and James and John the brother of James. When they came to the house of the ruler of the synagogue, he saw a tumult, and people weeping and wailing loudly. And when he had entered he said to them, 'Why do you make a tumult and weep? The child is not dead but sleeping.' And they laughed at him (Mark 5.35-40).

This story is Jesus' counterpart to the story of Abraham and Sarah. Just as God's announcement inevitably seemed laughable to the old Abraham and Sarah, so Jesus' announcement to the people round the synagogue provoked their mirth. It sounded laughable to Abraham and Sarah that God would create new life through them; it sounds laughable to Jesus' hearers that he could awaken the dead to life. Here Jesus appears as the foolishness of God incarnate, as the ridiculed preacher of the kingdom of God.

Jesus continues to be laughed at to the end. Even on the cross he evidently had to listen to laughing contemporaries – in particular the rulers among them – who inevitably felt the discrepancy between his beginnings and his end: 'He saved others; let him save himself, if he is the Christ of God, his chosen One' (Luke 23.35). So we will not go far wrong in interpreting Jesus like this: 'Jesus was neither a fool nor a rebel, but evidently open to confusion with both. In the end he was mocked by Herod as a fool and delivered over to the cross by his fellow-countrymen as a rebel.'[18] Significantly, one of the earliest 'depictions' of Jesus of Nazareth, a drawing scratched on stone, shows him hanging from the cross with an ass's head.[19]

The crucified Jesus as fool

No wonder, then, that this laughed-at Jesus has become the archetype for laughed-at believers. Moreover artists like James Ensor and George Rouault have with some justification depicted Jesus in the garb of a clown. They could not have described the deep significance of his life and ministry more aptly: 'Like the jester, Christ defies custom and scorns crowned heads. Like a wandering troubadour he has no place to lay his head. Like the clown in the circus parade he satirizes existing authority by riding into town replete with regal pageantry when he has no earthly power. Like a minstrel he frequents dinners and parties. At the end he is costumed by his enemies in a mocking caricature of royal paraphernalia. He is crucified amid sniggers and taunts with a sign over his head that lampoons his laughable claim' – thus the American theologian Harvey Cox aptly sums up the essentials.[20]

Nor is it coincidence that not only the graphic artists but also the artists with words were fascinated by Jesus as a clown, as a fool. Gerhart Hauptmann wrote a novel with the title *The Fool in Christ Emanuel Quint*, and Heinrich Böll gave his 'hero' Hans Schnier features of the foolish Nazarene in *Faces of a Clown*.[21] There are also paradoxical shifts here: Jesus – the man with a foolish message, who in the end stands there mocked. Jesus – the man from whom emanated a liberating message, but who in the end drew down upon himself the mockery of the pious. Heinrich Heine, the poet with experience of conflicts, instinctively recognized this:

> Each time with melancholy your countenance
> fills me, my sorry cousin,
> you who wanted to redeem the world,
> you fool, you saviour of mankind.
>
> They played an evil trick on you,
> those lords of the High Council,
> who made you speak so recklessly,
> of church and state?[22]

So at the end of the story of Jesus we do not have the image of a laughing God or a laughing saviour but the image of a laughed-at fool, who stands for God. At the end we have the stifled laugh, the killed-off joy; at the end we have the pain and crying of the executed man and the malice and mockery of the executioners. Here – in a comparison of religions – Christianity claims a distinctive feature.

For if I see it rightly, in none of the great religions do the profound and the comic, the exalted and the ridiculous, demolition and malice, faith and mockery, stand so close together as in Christianity, according to its most authentic sources. The account of the passion in the Gospel of Matthew illustrates this a most impressive way:

> And those who passed him by *derided him*, wagging their heads and saying, 'You who would destroy the temple and build it in three days, save yourself! If you are the *Son of God*, come down from the cross.' So also the chief priests, with the scribes and elders, *mocked* him, saying, 'He saved others, he cannot save himself. He is the *King of Israel*; let him come down now from the cross, and we will believe in him. He trusts in God: let God deliver him now, if he desires him; for he said, "I am *the Son of*

God." ' And the robbers who were crucified with him also *reviled* him in the same way (27.39-44).

The words in italics in this passage should make my concern clear. In one and the same text the great words, the deep confessions, are immersed in the twilight of the frivolous and mocking:

Son of God	– save yourself
King of Israel	– come down from the cross, if you can
Trust in God	– let him help him now.

So in one and the same text the startling and the laughable lie closely together. The son of God on the cross – what mockery! The king of Israel on the cross – what a joke! The preacher from Nazareth's trust in God – how comic and grotesque in view of such an end! In no comparable text of the great religions does one find such a combination of faith and mockery, confession and laughter.

But conversely that also means that Christian faith is always endangered, a faith which asserts itself through malice, mockery and wit. Tribulation follows it like a shadow. Mockery of such an 'impossible' faith is something that Christians have had to put up with from the beginning. Christian faith cannot avoid mockery; only on the other side of the laughter of doubters and mockers can it preserve and prove itself. So as those who are mocked, Christians will always take the side of the victims of mockery, in solidarity with those who are laughed at and trampled on. They will never forget that in his bitterest hour their master from Nazareth belonged among those who were laughed at, indeed that God made a fool of himself for our sake. They will combat this kind of laughter with resistance in the spirit.

It was not granted to Jesus, as it was to Buddha Gautama, to achieve perfection while he was still alive, to live in cheerful-earnest enlightenment, harmoniously and successfully, highly regarded by the powerful. It was not granted to Jesus in his lifetime to embody composure, inner peace, deep harmony of the kind that is rightly attributed to the Buddha and is visibly expressed by all the statues of the Buddha. The laughter of the Buddha has become a symbol of a redeemed cheerfulness, a silent joy, a purified harmony which anyone who follows Buddha can achieve here and now – on the presupposition of strict asceticism and meditation. The joy of Christians in the world and over the world has to be distinguished from that.

5. The Spirit of Joy

Jesus' joy was evidently indestructible, as is proved by the further history of his followers. And this indestructibility found its expression in belief in the resurrection of the crucified Jesus by God. In this way the earliest community expressed their conviction that lamentation and mourning do not have the last word.

Easter laughter at death

Here too the reports in the Gospels are not naively optimistic stories of joy. That the crucified Jesus is alive: how laughable that sounds! Let us follow Luke again, in particular his accounts of the events after the resurrection. Everywhere we come upon unbelief, scepticism, mistrust. The first witnesses to the empty tomb? The apostles regard it as 'gossip' (24.11). The first attempts by Peter to see for himself? 'Bewilderment' (24.12) – no more! No, at first Jesus' disciples do not understand anything (24.25). Why should they, when one reflects what a fiasco the cruel death of their master on the cross was? The risen Christ himself had to 'open their eyes' (on the way from Jerusalem to Emmaus) and tell them that the fate of the Messiah had to look like this: 'Thus it is written, that the Christ should suffer and on the third day rise from the dead, and that repentance and forgiveness of sins should be preached in his name to all nations, beginning from Jerusalem' (24.46f.). Indeed, the risen Christ has to send his despondent disciples the Holy Spirit, literally equip them 'with power from on high' (24.49), in order to liberate them from their depressions and despairs.

It is hardly possible to depict more vividly that belief in the resurrection of the crucified Jesus by God is humanly speaking an impossibility. It took 'power from on high' to turn doubt and scepticism into faith and trust. It took 'power from on high' to turn mourning into joy. Only at the end of this story, literally in the penultimate sentence of his Gospel, does Luke take up one of his basic themes again: messianic joy. Only now – when the disciples have understood the 'meaning' and received 'power from on high' – can they return to Jerusalem, enter the temple and praise God.

So the joy of Christians is anything but an optimism which suppresses problems. It is joy with a garland of mourning. It is joy with the cruel death of the cross behind it, joy which nurtures itself on nothing but the experience that the crucified Jesus did not remain in death but lives through God's action and remains alive in the Spirit. Only on the basis of this certainty can the Good Friday mourning be changed into ever-irrepressible Easter joy. Only in the light of this certainty can Christians. in faith in the resurrection of the crucified Jesus, laugh at death, that power which seems to be the strongest and bitterest on earth. That is the Christian parallel to Psalm 2: resurrection as an expression of God's laughter at death. And only in this way can we understand the cry of jubilation into which Paul breaks out in his First Letter to the Corinthians: 'Death is swallowed up in victory. Death, where is your sting? Grave, where is your victory?' (15.54f.). What is that if not Easter jubilation, Easter laughter?

Easter laughter at death! How little trace of that there still is in the churches! Here a look at history helps to break down constraints and to counter the deadly serious solemnity which has found its way into the liturgy of the churches. For in German-speaking countries for centuries preachers at the Easter mass used to provoke the congregation to violent bursts of laughter – not even being afraid of obscene pantomimes and *double entendres*. This was called *risus paschalis*, Easter laughter. It was an institution which persisted. In her book on *Easter Laughter. Sexuality and Pleasure in the Sphere of the Holy*, published in 1992, Maria Catherina Jacobelli has once again brought together abundant material on this.[23]

Here we find that perhaps the earliest document on Easter laughter so far known to us comes from the Basel reformer Oecolampadius (1482-1531), who comments critically on the tradition of Easter laughter in a letter *De risu paschali* from the year 1518, addressed to the Basel theologian Wolfgang Capito. This was still at a time when Oecolampadius, whose civic name was Johann Hausschein, was working as a Catholic priest in

Basel. Only in 1521/22 did he join the Reformation and with his enthusiastic addresses play a not insignificant part in making the city of Basel officially accept the Protestant faith.

The dispute over Easter laughter

What does this letter to Wolfgang Capito say? It is written in Oecolampadius's defence. For previously Capito had embarked on a wide-ranging criticism of his colleague's preaching style, the main point being that he was too serious. We know from another letter of Capito's that Oecolampadius had accepted this criticism: 'The reason (why Oecolampadius had been criticized) is that he did not terrify the loose women with his voice and wild gesticulation, either with invented threats or with Salmonic noise.[24] Instead of following the traditional pattern, he stubbornly refrains from these things, namely, telling stories and jokes which come from the kitchens. He does not incite the congregation to loud laughs while he preaches Christ; he does not jest with lewd words, nor does he call on them to imitate someone who is gratifying himself like a buffoon with the things which married people are accustomed to do in their bedrooms without witnesses.'

Now Capito wants Oecolampadius to do precisely this. Why? Because otherwise 'the preachers would speak to empty churches'. So he has no understanding of the earnestness of his colleague. Oecolampadius did not hesitate even to rebuke him 'above all for the inappropriate jests at the Easter celebration with which they (the preachers) banish in every way the piety and gratitude towards God that we should increase. As though it were only permissible to receive with buffoonery the risen Christ who suffered death for us.'

Oecolampadius continued to be nauseated by all these jests, jokes and smuttiness during the liturgy: 'And they (the preachers) are content only if they imitate the whole body of buffooneries and utter unwashed words full of shamelessness. It gets to the point that the preacher, like a travelling comedian, spends most of his time depicting every kind of abomination, thus forgetting his calling... Since I do not like this shamefulness, people think I am too earnest and absolutely ridiculous, whereas those who are for this frivolity are taken very seriously and are thought worthy of twofold honour.'

Basel was no exception. The Easter laughter was a widespread church custom in the sixteenth century which was even defended by representatives of the church (Capito at any rate was a priest and preacher at Basel Cathedral). It was regarded as a quite legitimate way of attracting people to church on Easter morning, and the sexual sphere was not tabu. The same goes for non-liturgical Easter celebrations, which similarly show that the Easter festival was the point at which the comic element broke into religion.

Here too Walter Haug has impressively summarized the literary evidence: 'Comedy also breaks out in the paraliturgical Easter celebration which depicts Mary's visit to the tomb. There is a series of episodes here which extend the celebration so that it becomes a play. First of all there are the scenes at the shop. The Maries buy unguents on their way to the tomb. Here there is an opportunity not only for haggling with the the old, mean Jewish shopkeeper but also for the staging of a burlesque adultery between his wife and the servant. Then the apostles' running to the tomb is turned into a comic race. Peter, who has to get there later, has to limp, as though he had a bad back, or he has fallen asleep, or he is generally lazy and can only keep going with vigorous gulps from his bottle. Then there is the appearance of Christ to Mary Magdalene. The Risen Christ appears as a gardener and plays tricks on her. He tells her off for walking on the plants. He suggests that she has a rendezvous in the garden with her lover, and so on. The scenes with the guards set over the tomb are even more turbulent. Here there are arguments over wages, and after the resurrection the soldiers get beaten because no one will accept blame for the catastrophe. But the wildest thing is the comic development of the descent of Christ into hell, a context in which it is possible to play out the most grotesque and lamentable impotence of the bands of demons.'[25]

Despite all the understandable criticism of the excesses, this Easter laughter remained in the liturgy even after the sixteenth century, though the obscene element increasingly faded into the background in the course of the next centuries. But the custom was still so widespread that even a handbook for preachers was printed, telling them how they could best get a laugh out of their people. This handbook has the *imprimatur* of the church, which shows that at least in some areas Easter laughter remained officially bound up with the Easter liturgy...[26]

And today? Why should this custom be completely banished from the churches? Why is laughter so tabu in the liturgy? Are Christians afraid of their own laughter or of the laughter of God? Or have they so little faith that they do not even have anything to laugh at? Do they believe that liturgy and laughter do not belong together, because God might find this offensive? How reduced a picture of God that would be! Wouldn't this be to confuse one's own morality with the living reality of God? Didn't the Christian Easter liturgy in particular from earliest times take up a saying from the psalms and relate it to the day of the resurrection of Jesus Christ: 'This is the day which the Lord has made; let us rejoice and be glad in it' (118.24)? But if this is to be more than a nice quotation, one might ask: what has become of jubilation and joy in today's liturgy?

The 'new existence' in the Spirit

At any rate the New Testament still knows Easter rejoicing, Easter laughter. It follows from this that Easter laughter will not cease as long as the message of the resurrection of the crucified Jesus is proclaimed. Where this laughter is suppressed – for whatever pious motives – death continues to prevail, that death the death of which is proclaimed at Easter. The death of the heart prevails. But the resurrection of Jesus Christ – as we learn especially from the apostle Paul – is the dawn of a great turning point: not only the messianic change of ages, the eschatological change from the old to the new creation, but also the great change of heart. According to Paul, Jesus' resurrection in fact at the same time means the exaltation of Jesus Christ to be Lord of the world (Philippians 2.6-11). Jesus Christ now lives in God's mode of being, the mode of being of the Spirit, as Lord in the Spirit. To put it in our language: Jesus Christ is abidingly present among us, effectively active, as the spiritual energy of God. Only in this way can a change of heart come about, in the Spirit. Anyone who lives in this spirit of Christ is, according to Paul, a new existence, a new creation (II Corinthians 5.17).[27]

For Paul, joy is an indissoluble part of the signature of the 'new creation': despite everything that Christians have behind them and before them. According to Paul, Christians have every reason to rejoice, because they owe their new existence not to themselves but to Christ. In precisely what does this 'new creation' consist? It consists in a new freedom (II Corinthians 3.17), freedom from the 'works of the law', the 'works of the flesh' (Galatians 5.19-21) and freedom for the 'works of the Spirit'. What are these works of the Spirit? According to Paul:

> Love, joy, peace, patience, kindness, goodness, faithfulness, gentleness, self-control. Against these there is no law. And those who belong to Christ Jesus have crucified the flesh with its passions and desires. If we live by the Spirit, let us also walk by the Spirit. Let us have no self-conceit, no provoking of one another, no envy of one another (Galatians 5.22-26).

Already in Paul this 'joy in the Holy Spirit' (Romans 14.17) which is grounded in Christ has nothing to do with cheap optimism, with suppressing problems or passing over the conflicts of the world. In their joy Christians do not live outside the conflicts but in them, do not live with their backs to the problems but confronting them. A man like Paul in particular knew that joy is to be had only in and through tribulation. As he can write to his Corinthians: 'Despite all our affliction, I have great pride in you; I am filled with joy' (II Corinthians 7.4). Despite all our affliction...

In other words, a theology of joy would be nothing but a naive suppression of reality were it not mediated critically through a theology of suffering. And a theology of suffering is at the same time a theology of arguing with God, of protest, lamentation and complaint. The question of theodicy remains the constant tribulation for a Christian joy which may be certain of the 'new creation' in Jesus Christ. It is worth recalling here what I myself said in a published discussion with my Tübingen colleague Walter Gross on the question 'Is God responsible for evil?': there can be no theology of joy without a theology of the cross, but conversely there can be no theology of the cross without a theology of joy. The two theologies are not mutually exclusive, but condition each other.[28] That is what comprises Christian foolishness. Christian foolishness?

6. The Christian as a Fool

No one was clearer than Paul that the Christian message of the 'new creation' made possible by the cross and resurretion must seem to non-Christians sheer folly, utter foolishness. To believe that the cross is not just to be seen as a fiasco but rather that it has a 'meaning', a purpose of God with human beings, is already too much to ask – for Gentiles or for Jews. Paul knew that when he attempted to make the word of the cross comprehensible to his community in Corinth:

> For the word of the cross is folly to those who are perishing, but to us who are being saved it is the power of God. For it is written, 'I will destroy the wisdom of the wise, and the cleverness of the clever I will thwart.' Where is the wise man? Where is the scribe? Where is the debater of this age? Has not God made foolish the wisdom of the world? For since, in the wisdom of God, the world did not know God through wisdom, it pleased God through the folly of what we preach to save those who believe. For Jews demand signs and Greeks seek wisdom, but we preach Christ crucified, a stumbling block to Jews and folly to Gentiles, but to those who are called, both Jews and Greeks, Christ the power of God and the wisdom of God. For the foolishness of God is wiser than men, and the weakness of God is stronger than men (I Corinthians 1.18-25).

The 'fool in Christ' corresponds to the fool Christ himself. In discipleship of Christ, Christians also become fools, because from the perspective of the non-believer there is something 'impossible', 'comic', 'offensive' about their faith.

The foolishness of God

But the deepest foundation for the foolishness of Christians lies in the 'foolishness of God' himself. It is God himself who not only unmasks the wisdom of the world as folly but has also chosen what is foolish in the world, i.e. makes himself known through what is foolish, makes the foolish the means of his initiative of salvation. It is God himself who with the resurrection of the crucified Jesus unhinges the criteria for human wisdom and thus exposes himself to the mockery of the so-called 'wise'. According to Paul, Christians have to do with a God who is not afraid of mockery and who voluntarily exposes himself to laughter. The God who is recognized in the crucified Christ is therefore the one who is laughed at, scorned and mocked. This is the deepest reason why Christians always look on idle, heedless, mocking laughter with mistrust and resist the demon which is released in this laughter. Because God in Christ himself was among those who have been laughed at, Christians will always take the side of those who are laughed at, indeed will grant the ridiculed and the mocked their dignity and rights 'for God's sake'. In a word, for Christians, knowledge of God and foolishness, discipleship of Christ and folly, belong indissolubly together.

Paul, too, was aware that discipleship of Christ and folly belong together. His gripping 'fool's speech' (in II Corinthians) makes this clear. Here Paul is reflecting one of the most serious situations in his life:

I repeat, let no one think me foolish; but even if you do, accept me as a fool, so that I too may boast a little. (What I am saying I say not with the Lord's authority but as a fool, in this boastful confidence; since many boast of worldly things, I too will boast.) For you gladly bear with fools, being wise yourselves! For you bear it if a man makes slaves of you, or preys upon you, or takes advantage of you, or puts on airs, or strikes you in the face. To my shame, I must say, we were too weak for that.

But whatever anyone dares to boast of – I am speaking as a fool – I also dare to boast of that. Are they Hebrews? So am I. Are they descendants of Abraham? So am I. Are they servants of Christ? I am a better one – I am talking like a madman – with far greater labours, far more imprisonments, with countless beatings, and often near death. Five times I have received at the hands of the Jews the forty lashes less one. Three times I have been beaten with rods; once I was stoned. Three times I have been shipwrecked; a night and a day I have been adrift at sea; on frequent journeys, in danger from rivers, danger from robbers, danger from my own people, danger from Gentiles, danger in the city, danger in the wilderness, danger at sea, danger from false brethren; in toil and hardship, through many a sleepless night, in hunger and thirst, often without food, in cold and exposure. And, apart from other things, there is the daily pressure upon me of my anxiety for all the churches. Who is weak, and I am not weak? Who is made to fall, and I am not indignant? If I must boast, I will boast of the things that show my weakness (11.16-10).

So when Paul speaks of a 'joy in the holy Spirit' grounded in Christ, he does so in awareness of the dialectic of wisdom and folly. No one was more aware than he of how endangered Christian existence is and how much joy in Christ goes with suffering for Christ's sake. But it is the spirit of joy which makes Christians capable of living in the world without being oppressed by the contradictions of the world and swallowed up in its abysses. For Paul this joy is a way of co-existence in the world with all its contradictions, without fully surrendering to the structure of this world, a way of transcending one's own situation without being insensitive to its scandals.

The Protestant theologian Jürgen Moltmann has aptly described this basic Pauline notion in his *Theology and Joy*: 'Resurrection and *Easter freedom* have the cross of Christ behind them, and the physical end of the law, of regimentation and death in the world, still before them. So Easter freedom does not permit us to escape from the world or to forget about it. Rather it leads us critically to accept the world situation with its unacceptable moments and *patiently to bring about change in the world* so that it may become a place of freedom for men and women. Thus both the laughter of Easter and the sorrow of the cross are alive in liberated men and women. They are not only laughing with those who laugh and weeping with those who weep, as Paul proposes in Romans 12.15, but they are also laughing with the weeping and weeping with the laughing as the Beatitudes of Jesus recommended. Their game always points critically at the oppressors. It therefore constantly provokes harassment by those who prohibit laughter because they fear liberty.'[29]

But are not joy and laughter two different things? Certainly. And there has often been an argument as to whether laughter is to be explained from joy or joy from laughter. For the New Testament it is clear that the foundation of Christian existence is the new joy made possible in the 'event of Jesus Christ' in and to God and the world, a joy which need not always express itself in laughter, but which becomes concrete in laughter. Furthermore, without it the ambiguity of laughter could not have a clear ethical qualification.

In other words, it is only in the light of a theology of joy in God and human beings that a Christian theology of laughter is justified, indeed can first be unmistakably defined in ambivalent human laughter: if laughter does not have the character of mockery, of malice, of contempt or exclusion, but has the character of liberated and redeemed joy which breaks down barriers and brings integration. So Christians do not have to ask whether they may laugh before God, at God or at human beings; they only have to ask in what spirit they are laughing. The laughter of Christians is laughter in the spirit of the crucified Jesus of Nazareth and his beatitudes, beatitudes which are addressed precisely to the despised and persecuted, beatitudes which change hearts – in the awareness that laughing Christians can at the same moment belong with those who are laughed at, like their master from Nazareth.

That is why there are always two sides to a Christian theology of laughter: there is a laughter of happiness and joy at God, especially in the interests of those who are marginalized and excluded, which derives its credentials and its unique character from the belief that God himself can laugh with the doubters and the despairing (Abraham and Sarah), and has more joy over a sinner who repents than over dozens of righteous who do not think that they need repentance. This laughter expresses the trust that God as proclaimed by Jesus of Nazareth has not 'become unaccustomed to laughter', as the Mephistopheleses of world history constantly suggest, because they hold against God the mercilessness and hopelessness of his creation. Rather, it is a sign of confidence that Christians have to do with a God who – as already in the case of Sarah and Abraham – also puts up with all human doubt in the meaning of his creation and promise and can change this in the end into a shared smile of happiness. It is laughter in trust that God's laughter is not devastating laughter, a laughter which threatens exclusion, but a laughter of boundless goodness and a joy in his creation and his creatures which cannot be disappointed.

The risk of being laughed at is the other side of a Christian theology of laughter. Anyone who in the spirit of the Sermon on the Mount believes in the possibility of changing human beings and the structures which alienate them, anyone who is not prepared to regard discipleship of Christ as a state of pious self-deception, should not be amazed that Jesus' description in the Sermon on the Mount already applies to them: 'Reviled and persecuted and with all kinds of evil said against you falsely on my account' (Matthew 5.11). Beyond question this happens in a subtler way today. Still a Christian? A weary wink, a malicious grin, a superior smile, a barbed indication of having seen through you... These are forms of being laughed at: the price of laughing with the laughing God.

And because Christians, like their master from Nazareth, time and again belong among those who are laughed at, without any moralizing finger-pointing they will combat the demon of a particular form of laughter: the laughter from above downwards, the demon of malice, of mockery, of laughing at those who in any case are weak and socially stigmatized. Their laughter remains bound once and for all to the humanity of Jesus. Laughter and ethical self-control belong indissolubly together for Christians. We shall have to look at this further in the last part of this book.

IV

Learning to Laugh: A Literary and Theological Tableau

1. Mozart's Laughter

Joyful laughter as a form of life, as an art of survival: what Jesus and Paul laid down the foundations for has been made clear to us contemporaries of the late twentieth century in its own way by a novel of world literature. This is Hermann Hesse's *Steppenwolf*, which was published in 1926.[1] Hardly any other novel in German literature portrays so scrupulously the inner split and division in modern men and women: the way in which they fall victim to their drives, their potential for destruction through modern technology, their neurotic impulses towards fulfilment, their ivory-tower intellectualism, their moral unscrupulousness. *Steppenwolf* is a novel which inexorably holds up a mirror to the men and women of the late twentieth century and in so doing confronts them with the truth about themselves. The hero of this novel, Harry Haller, is unrestrainedly to 'learn to listen to more of the radio music of life'.[2]

What the Steppenwolf had to learn

And yet at the end of this novel we do not have not the suicide of the inwardly torn intellectual analyst who is unfit for life. At the end of the novel we have the figure of the 'laughing Mozart', who belongs to the world of the 'immortals'. Hesse himself wanted people not to overlook, for all the problems, 'a second, higher, imperishable world' in his Steppenwolf. The world of the Steppenwolf's suffering is contrasted with 'a positive, cheerful, suprapersonal and supratemporal world of faith as it is embodied, say, in the music of Wolfgang Amadeus Mozart'.[3] Moreover it is Mozart who explains in a visionary appearance to the hero of this novel:

94

'You are to live and to learn to laugh. You are to listen to life's radio music and to reverence the spirit behind it and to laugh at the bim-bim in it. So there you are. More will not be asked of you.'[4]

If we follow this novel, for people of the late twentieth century, who have experienced or tried everything, laughter is no longer spontaneous or natural, but has become a task of life, literally the art of spiritual survival. And indeed only at the end does the hero of Steppenwolf understand that the way out is not suicide but laughter, and learn what the meaning of this laughter can be: to find a form of existence in the world without simply adapting to this world or disparaging it. Harry Haller and with him the men and women of the twentieth century must understand that there must be a laughing relationship to this disintegrating split world which does not suppress the conflicts or experience this world merely as a trap. This laughter would be a way of seeing through the world without disparaging it, living in the world and yet not falling victim to its structures, co-existing with the split without simply confirming the *status quo*. Laughter would be a way of non-regressive reconciliation with one's own finitude and divided nature. How had the hero of Steppenwolf described himself in the 'Treatise on the Steppenwolf'?

> The lone wolves who know no peace... for them is reserved, provided suffering has made their spirits tough and elastic enough, a way of reconcilement and escape into humour... Humour alone, that magnificent discovery of those who are cut short in their calling to highest endeavour, those who falling short of tragedy are yet as rich in gifts as in affliction, humour alone (perhaps the most inborn and brilliant achievement of the human spirit) attains to the impossible and brings every aspect of human existence within the ray of its prism. To live in the world as though it were not the world, to respect the law and yet to stand above it, to have possessions as though 'one possessed nothing', to renounce as though it were no renunciation, all these favourite and often formulated propositions of an exalted worldly wisdom, it is in the power of humour alone to make efficacious.[5]

The allusions to a saying of the apostle Paul are unmistakable: 'I mean that the appointed time has grown very short; from now on, let those who have wives live as though they had none, and those who mourn as though they were not mourning, and those who rejoice as though they were not rejoicing, and those who buy as though they had no goods, and those who deal with the world as though they had no dealings with it. For the form of this world is passing away' (I Corinthians 7.29). What Paul is describing here is the signature of human existence in a world which will soon pass away. In this fleeting, transitory world a Christian can live without comfortably adjusting to it, but also without denouncing it, disparaging it or apocalyptically wishing for its downfall. Christians can live in a fragile balance, which is in danger at all times, between involvement and relaxation, commitment and *laissez faire*, concern and cheerfulness. In one of his most impressive texts, which also has an autobiographical colouring, Paul, who is sore tried but not resigned, once again described this existential dialectic of the Christian like this: 'We are treated as impostors, and yet are true; as unknown, and yet well known; as dying, and behold we live; as punished, and yet not killed; as sorrowful, yet always rejoicing: as poor, yet making many rich; as having nothing, and yet possessing everything' (II Corinthians 6.8-10). Joyful at all times? How can we translate this statement today?

Laughter as resistance

If the joy in God and human beings made possible by Christ is not in our day to lead to pious self-deception about the state of the world (for us with Auschwitz, Hiroshima and the Gulag Archipelago round our necks), a theology of joy can only be conceived of as a criticism of ideology, as a form of spiritual resistance, in two directions:
• as resistance against those who happily suppress problems, who live out their Christian joy with no concern for the empirical state of creation and purchase their pious cheerfulness at the cost of overlooking things. But also
• as resistance against the humourless apostles of catastrophe who love to conclude from partial experiences of catastrophe that all creation is fallen and ripe for apocalyptic destruction.

A theology of joy understood in these terms makes even laughter possible. And laughter in a spirit of joy is an expression of a

96

capacity for a de-fanaticizing and self-relativizing of political fantasies or a religious determination for truth. In joyful laughter at the state of the world, on whose stage the same tragicomedies seem to have been playing for ages, we can achieve self-relativizing, self-critical detachment *coram deo*, which in our century can be literally necessary for the spiritual art of survival. Laughter at the state of the church leads to a liberating disclosure of what is all too human in it, and encourages one to stay and not to go. Indeed in terms of system theory, laughter is an indissoluble part of an organism like the church and is inseparable from its 'nature': 'The fact that any system of thought has its specific norms also excludes anything specific, and therefore it develops a specific comedy of its own. Only the terrorist system has no comedy, because it radically suppresses what it excludes; it prevents self-relativizing with violence and therefore must do everything possible to wall up the most vulnerable point of entry, comedy.'[6]

2. Tucholsky's Laughter

But this laughter does not apply only to the church. It also applies to God's creation generally. For a theology of laughter in the spirit of joy is no contradiction to doubt in God and his creation. Nor is it a contradiction to listening tö *God's* doubt in his creatures. I would like to demonstrate both these aspects from probably the greatest satirist and political journalist of twentieth-century German literature, Kurt Tucholsky (1890-1935).

Laughter at the comic side of creatures

Kurt Tucholsky gave expression to God's laughter at his creatures in a witty poem of social criticism. It bears the title 'Brief Conversation with an Unexpected Outcome'.

The Lord God sat on a cushion of clouds
and looked at his earth.
What's that noise down there?
Look, it's an aeroplane.

An officer greets him with a friendly smile:
'If I may, Swabia number four!'
and the propellers whirr aloud,

'Now we're here.'

'What have you to say about our victory?
We broke the record in the games.
Why? We need it for war...'
'For war? For murder?'

'Excuse me, you're too feeble.'
'And who gave you that much money?'
'The people! It was mostly the people,
from the Rhine to the Belt.'

'The people? Do they have such crooked necks?
Are your people so stupid?'
Here God laughed with bulging cheeks.
He toppled over.[7]

Human beings – this is the starting point of this poem – are childishly proud of their technical achievements, their victories and records. In their naivety they regard even a plane as nothing but a toy for war, without noticing what they are really doing. So in this poem Tucholsky is mocking a humanity which has not yet seen through its potential for self-destruction, and takes the side of a 'God' (here of course as a mythical quotation) who speaks plainly (war is murder) and laughs at human beings in their arrogant ignorance. God laughs at the stupidity of a people which still puts at the disposal of its rulers and those in power means which they misuse for waging war.

Here the poem speculates in a refined dialectical way on the proud reaction of the people, who do not really want to be 'stupid' and who want to get rid of the passion for war among those in power. With political and strategic calculation it presupposes that what the people fears most is God's laughter at its stupidity, so that in the end the people will burst out laughing at those in power. As the dramatist Friedrich Dürrenmatt, who had a good deal of experience in this area, also said: 'Human freedom manifests itself in laughter; and human distress in weeping. Today we have to show freedom. The tyrants of this planet are not touched by the works of the poets: they yawn at their laments; they regard their heroic songs as silly fairy-tales, they go to sleep during their religious poems: they fear only one thing, their mockery.[8]

Anyone who wants to know how bitter the laughter of human beings over the state of creation can be should join Kurt Tucholsky in the school of laughter. Above all in his short dialogue sketches, entitled *Afterwards*, which begin in 1925 and extend over a period of three years, Tucholsky reflected increasingly deeply on the meaning of his existence as a contemporary and as a writer – hovering, as was typical of him, between cheerfulness and melancholy, irony and earnest. It is no coincidence that as a pseudonym for these *Afterwards* pieces he used the name Kaspar Hauser, the stranger who understood the world as little as his *alter ego* in the twentieth century.

These prose sketches are daydreams of a life 'afterwards', after death. The author fantasizes in the midst of life about a state after life, in order to be able to look back from the life 'afterwards' to life 'before'. Tucholsky would not have been a satirist who delighted in literary effect had he not used the opportunity to adorn this life after death with the parody of clichés about the life to come. He clearly enjoyed playing with mythical substitutes, contradicting fantasies of heaven, making fun of images of God in ironic brokenness. Two men are sitting in a heavenly bath or on a cloud and dangling their legs. They comment in delight on the inauguration of a new planet, the closing festival on a satellite moon, a masked ball on the Milky Way. Odd spirits fly past, presumably on their way to a spiritualist session. There are constant showers of meteors, punctuated by the roaring of acoustic primal mud, and matter groans away. God himself has become 'a cross between a heavenly bookkeeper and an eccentric modeller': an 'old gentleman' who sometimes organizes a meteor shower for a change and on whom one can play tricks: 'We made gestures at Him in his storm and He was quite desperate.'[9]

Tucholsky does not take the opportunity here, as elsewhere in his work, to show his talent as a comedian, to put into practice his delight in having fun with parody and playing with traditions (above all religious traditions) like a child playing with the bones of a skeleton. And yet here the game has an inscrutable character which soon makes the laughter stick in the reader's throat. For all the heavenly scenery is simply constructed in order to offer a view of human life as a whole, its roles and poses, its anxieties and longings. Here Tucholsky is not staging a farewell to a ridiculous pompous God with crude effects, but is seeing through human beings, showing up their attitudes and masks. The *Afterwards* pieces are simply unsparing interim reports of the thirty-five year-old writer on the meaning of the life he has lived so far, and these interim reports sound bitter: 'Seventy-two years on earth,' Tucholsky makes one of his conversation partners say. 'That means having lied for sixty-nine years, having hidden one's feelings, been hypocritical, grinned instead of biting, taunted where one has loved... Sometimes one has an inkling that it would be better to stop.'[10]

What is left for human beings? At any rate there is laughter. And it is no coincidence that one of the closing scenes of the *Afterwards* pieces is devoted to laughter. Where does laughter come from? Tucholsky has sketched out mythical scenery: laughter comes from the 'Mount of Laughter', a volcano from which laughter erupts and falls down on earth:

It was already dark when we stood before the gigantic mountain. 'What's that? Where are you taking me?' he asked gently. 'It's the Mount of Laughter. Come a bit closer, up here. Can you hear?' We listened.

Cascades of laughter came rumbling out, waves of laughter, streams of giggles, whole scales rattled down, great feet coming down staircases towards us, and when they got down, they ebbed away breathlessly into little sounds... The ground moved gently under our feet. The basses laughed with a dull drone; trills of female laughter arose and fell melodiously down, coloratura laughter and silver bells. The laughter of *Schaden-freude* waltzed oilily down and broke noisily on the shore; cackles of laughter and the joyful laughter of children, sharp laughing voices which came down headlong, each tumbling over the other, then they all collapsed. And again a chorus of laughter arose, dully drowned by a thick, old voice, accompanied by a sweet woman's voice. Silence. A rivulet of tears of laughter dropped by us.

'That's the volcano of laughter,' I said. 'Didn't you know it? You've shown me so much up here and didn't you know it? It provides laughter for those down below; it drops from above, it rolls out of the crater of the volcano, all kinds. All the laughter there is. Have you heard it? Grins and whistling whips with little knots in the lash, they burn so beautifully... stupid laughter and liberating laughter and bonbons of laughter filled with tears – all that comes from there. But you can't get up.'

'What's up there?' he asked. 'I've been told,' I said, 'that there's a gigantic hole deep as Etna, and it flows out of there.' – 'But where does it come from?' he asked. 'Who provides the earth with laughter – where does this huge quantity of laughter come from, so inexhaustible, the perpetual readiness to give and to give?'

'There is a thing,' I said, 'which has understood why He has created it, down there. He has understood the joke of the world. Since then...' 'Since then?' he asked. 'Since then the thing has been laughing,' I said.

We turned away. Far below us we saw the two fall, to their private hell. 'A strange business,' I said. He wanted to laugh, suddenly stopped. In the darkness an animal soul shyly slipped past us. 'Has that never drunk from the brook of tears of laughter?', he asked. 'Animals don't laugh,' I said. 'They are nature itself, which is earnest, inexorable – perhaps cheerful – but laugh? It doesn't laugh.' 'And why not?' he said. 'Because it's afraid,' I said. 'It's afraid that one might be laughing at him. No one does that here. They go to the Mount of Laughter and laugh, but only to one another. Can you hear how it's coming down?

Now the whole mountain was showered with laughter, falling and rising; first we laughed with it a little, then we kept on laughing, and now it sounded very sad. 'Laughter is a concession of the Lord,' I said. 'And also afterwards,' he said. Then we slid down.[11]

This story is ambiguous: the source of laughter – we learn – is a 'thing' which has understood the 'joke of the world', in other words has understood why God created the world at all. And at the same time we learn that this laughter is a concession of this very God to human beings. If we isolate what the statement is actually saying from this mythical garb, Tucholsky's readers are confronted with a primal paradox of their existence: the contradictions in creation are so great that only laughter remains;

indeed laughter seems to be the automatic consequence of perceiving these contradictions. But this capacity for laughter is at the same time one granted by God to human beings, so that they can live with the contradictions, so that they can achieve a tolerable coexistence in this world.

3. Freud's Laughter

Laughter as an expression of the comedy of creation. This is also the starting point of the jokes which are widespread throughout Christianity and Judaism. What would the church be without the numerous jokes about theologians, clergy and popes? It would be unbearable. One does not need to have studied Sigmund Freud's famous 1905 study of *Jokes and Their Relation to the Subconscious* to be able to understand how liberating the power of the joke can be, particularly within an institution like the church. Nevertheless it is worth recalling Freud's basic thoughts about the psycho-social function of jokes.[12]

What jokes do

Freud's investigation of jokes had been preceded by his 1900 pioneering work on the interpretation of dreams. It had become clear to Freud that both dream and joke basically 'function' by analogous rules. The psychological processes which take place in the creation of a dream correspond to those in a joke. In both not only is there an analogous process of 'concentration', i.e. combining opposites in the smallest possible third common factor, in plays on words and dream languages. Similar drives are also involved: like the dream, the 'tendentious joke' (to be distinguished from word-play), which extends from dirty stories to cynicism, can also be understood as a pleasant wish-fulfilment. For a moment there is a release of repressed drives, not ciphered in the unconscious as in the case of a dream, but openly and publicly. It is the tendentious joke in particular which rebels against the pressures of thought and reality, which fights against 'reason – critical judgment – suppression', avoids repressions, and 'opens up new sources of pleasure for itself by lifting inhibitions'.[13]

And laughter? According to Freud, people laugh because 'a

sum of psychical energy which has hitherto been used for cathexis is allowed free discharge'.[14] Accordingly, laughter makes use of the element of psychical energy which has been released by the abolition of repression. Laughter is an expenditure of saved-up repression! In short, by laughing people unburden themselves – if only for a short time – of the effort of repression and playfully become open to new sources of pleasure: the censorship of their own inward life is temporarily distracted.

Even if one is neither a follower of Freudian psychoanalysis nor regards Freud's theory of laughter as comprehensive enough (why should the surplus of psychical energy which accumulates through the saving of repressions be discharged only in laughter?), Freud's observation is still incontrovertible in the case of certain forms of laughter caused by jokes. In fact the joke can disclose our most secret wishes, rid us of some of our moral inhibitions, make us conscious of some of our repressions and tabus, the precautions by which we live and under which we suffer. A joke can unburden us – and if we did not unburden ourselves, often we could not take the pressure, discharge aggression, without perhaps being inclined to violent actions.

In other words, the joke is similarly a form of coexistence with a world under whose contradictions we suffer without really being able to change them. It can reduce anxiety without completely removing it, express forbidden things without fully breaking with the dominaint structure of the world, provide relief without making everything a matter of indifference. The joke sharply brings out the discrepancy between what is and what should be, being and appearance, reality and fiction. It can be the role into which one slips in order to be able to tell others the truth without danger. It is often the disguise of the impotent, an evocation of the unexpected, a play on the repressive seriousness of a group or society, the widening of frontiers for a moment. In short, the joke sets the narrative scene for the cheerful acceptance of sorrow about the antinomies and aporias of existence, a form of non-regressive reconciliation with the contradictions in ourselves and the creation in which we live. In telling jokes one detaches oneself from a fixation on the merely problematical and shows the possibility of taking the poison out of an oppressive situation in the act of laughing and in this way coping with it psychologically.

The stronger the tabus, the more attractive it is to break them. The more rigid the bars, the more pleasant it is to rattle them. So it is no coincidence that jokes especially flourish in the sphere of religion. Christianity and Judaism are particularly affected by this. Jokes about them are legion. Here a few:

1. *Creation joke*: 'God created the world in only seven days,' says the theologian. The layman retorts, 'It looks like it.'

2. *Clergy joke*: 'How is it,' a Bishop of London once asked a famous actor, 'that we preachers usually make little impression with the lofty and true subjects that we proclaim, whereas you actors move people on the stage so much with your fictions?' The actor replied, 'It is because we speak of fictititous things as though they were true, whereas the clergy talk about true things as though they were fictitious.'[15]

3. *Pope joke*: One day the Lord God appeared privately to John Paul II in his private chapel in Rome during a mass. For months complaints had been reaching the Lord of the world from all points of the compass, above all about the impasse over the ordination of women, celibacy and the pill, and he had begin to get tired of them. But since he had handed over rule of the church to his representative on earth, he could do nothing without him. 'I would like to ask you,' said God the Lord, 'will the ordination of women be introduced during your lifetime?' The Pope replied, 'Not in my lifetime.' – 'Will you abolish the law of celibacy during your lifetime?' Again the Pope replied energetically, 'Not in my lifetime.' – 'But at least you will allow women the pill?' asked God the Lord in deep resignation. But the Pope remained inexorable, 'Not in my lifetime.' God was about to turn away, when the Pope himself took the initiative. 'While you're there, Almighty and Omniscient One, may I ask you to answer a question which has been tormenting me for a long time.' 'What is it?' 'Will there be another Polish pope after my death?' Like a shot God the Lord answered, 'Not in my lifetime!'

By contrast, Jewish jokes are often very profound. In addition to the experience of contrast and incongruity they also have a distinctive melancholy, 'something like sorrow that claim and reality evidently never coincide and that at least in order to get by one has to play games with the truth'.[16] That becomes particularly clear from the numerous jokes about the relationship between Jews and Christians. Each of these jokes reminds one how much Christianity poses as the religion of the victors, as the religion of the powerful, which does all it can to discriminate against Jews, to trick them and even to liquidate them. The Jewish theologian Salcia Landmann has made one of the most extensive collection of Jewish jokes about Christians.[17] Here are some examples.

1. *A pastor*: 'There are three things I can't stand about you Jews: the way you wander around in the synagogue in such an undisciplined way, your noisy prayer and your disorderly funerals.' The Jew: 'We wander around in the synagogue because we feel at home there. We pray loudly because our God is old and hard of hearing. And as for funerals, I too prefer the Christian ones.'

2. *A priest and a rabbi* are sitting in a train. The priest remarks, 'Last night I dreamed about the Jewish paradise. It was full of dirt and rubbish and very noisy.' The rabbi: 'How true. I too dreamed of paradise last night, but I dreamed about the Christian paradise. A splendid place, full of flowers, scents and sunshine. But not a soul to be seen.'

It's clear that such jokes in an unchallenged way lay bare and shatter Christian prejudices (the disorderly, noisy Jews). The open or latent triumphalism of Christianity is brought crashing down with a single joke. Jokes function as needles which burst blown-up balloons. In a flash, many of these Jewish jokes make Christians aware that their way of dealing with the Jewish people is not only arrogant, but is literally deadly serious. Christian statements about Jews often echo the astonishment that this people is stil alive, though for so long the church has been 'the only institution which brings salvation' and has replaced Israel. It is understandable that Jews need jokes to guarantee their survival, jokes which often originated in misery, expulsion and pogroms. Moreover Jewish jokes often have a tragic background, point to the grotesque and tragi-comic. Salcia Landmann rightly speaks of a 'double function of the joke which is usually clearly recognized by all masters of violence: on the one hand it is revolutionary, expresses repudiation and mistrust, and on the other it paralyses revolutionary plans because laughter relaxes and removes tension. It is the weapon of the defenceless, who moan but are half content with their lot.'[18]

Other Jewish jokes are the expression of an unshakeable self-confidence nurtured by the certainty of ultimately being the older and more worthy religion compared with Christianity. The most senior representatives of Christianity seem particularly comical and ridiculous against this background, as a joke about a papal visit to Jerusalem clearly shows: 'The mayor handed His Holiness a very old parchment. Despite their profound knowledge neither the Pope nor his entourage could decipher it. They asked the mayor what it was. "It's the bill for the last supper, still not paid. Could Your Holiness please settle it?"[19]

A third variant of Jewish jokes about Christianity is based on the effect that Christianity is not a special religion but a species of Judaism. Such jokes show up the Christian awareness of exclusiveness, just as they 'comfort' the Jews that in the end there is nothing special about being a Christian; it corresponds to the fate of God himself, who similarly lost his son to the Christians. 'My son has become a Christian.' 'So what did you do?' 'I complained about it to God.' 'And what did he say?' 'That it happened to his son too. I should do what he did.' 'And what did he do?' 'He said he immediately made a new testament.'[20]

Laughter as trust in God?

The reason why such jokes can function in the religious sphere, i.e. why they do not make the religious element disappear but bring out its deeper levels, is that they leave intact the reality of the God who is always greater. Laughter and trust in God are not opposites. Rather, laughter is participation in the laughter of God himself or trusting anticipation of God's possible laughter, it being presupposed or expected that God laughs or will laugh at the same comic things that we do. This is where a theology of laughter derives its credentials from – from the laughter of God himself. Jokes, irony and laughter are different stylistic means of relativizing all manmade religious institutions, claims and moralisms in the light of the God who is always greater. Those who laugh at such jokes are not remote from God, wicked and sinful, as certain psalms claim. There is also 'wicked' laughter for the sake of the greater God, a 'sin' against constricting God and making God a function of a particular religious system.

So as human efforts or institutions, theology and church are governed by a single all-decisive proviso: the proviso that they may possibly be the objects of divine laughter. They are warned by the experience of God which is expressed in Psalm 2 not to expose themselves to God's mockery through their praxis, since that would be worse than all human laughter put together. Theology and church have nothing more to fear than God's doubt in them, which is concentrated in the statement, 'But he who is enthroned in heaven laughs, the Lord mocks them.'

4. The Laughter of the Sad Princess

The ancients already knew that the human being is an *animal ridens*, a being who laughs. Human beings can laugh, and what can laugh is human. But laughter is more than a distinguishing feature of human beings. It goes deeper. For a particular laugh can first make a person a person, i.e. bring out his or her humanity. Certainly laughter can be the expression of a human crisis, as a form of alienation from oneself, above all in sick, demonic laughter. But there is also reconciling, healing, therapeutic laughter. Laugh yourself healthy! It is worth going into this therapeutic function of laughter. I have chosen the narrative form.

The healing power of laughter: two fairy tales

Short stories, and popular fairy tales in particular, often contain deep truth. They include folk tales. These contain little information but much orientation, little knowledge but much wisdom; little that is artificial but instead elementary instruction on life. Moreover many stories indicate a successful course from constraint to openness, from inertia to initiative, from having privileges to receiving gifts. Often it is not the strongest and the wisest who are the happiest in the end, but the weakest and most stupid. In many cases happiness proves not to be a merit but a gift, unmerited grace. Ernst Bloch once clear-sightedly put it like this: 'These fairy tales of the rebellion of the little folk against the mythical powers are like that; they are the Tom Thumbs of reason against the giants. Only a roving nature makes room here for another life than the one into which one was born, banished, or drawn. Instead of fate a story begins, Cinderella becomes a princess, the bold tailor wins the king's daughter.'[21]

That is what also happens in a fairy tale about a 'sad princess'. Ludwig Bechstein (1801-1860) handed it down in his collection of fairy tales, under the title 'Stick, Swan', as did the Brothers Grimm in their collection, under the title 'The Golden Goose'. The main character (here I shall keep to the simple story in the Bechstein tradition, which differs in many details from the Grimm version) is Gottfried, the youngest and weakest of three brothers who – as the stories now have it – suffered bitterly at the hands of his brothers. However, one day he meets an old woman 'in the wood' (fairy tales also like that) and she shows him a way out of his misery. She advises him to get a swan, which is not of course a normal swan. For when people touch it, at the cry 'Stick, swan', they stick to it. At the same time the woman tells the youth:

> When you've caught a pretty procession of human birds, just lead them straight on. Then you'll come to a big city in which there lives a princess who has never laughed. If you get her to laugh, your happiness is made.[22]

Of course things work out, and soon a grotesque and comic procession forms of people all now sticking to the swan. And above all the decisive thing happens:

> Gottfried could already see the towers of the capital ahead when a marvellous carriage came towards him with a beautiful, young, but serious lady sitting in it. But when she saw the strange procession she burst into loud laughter and her servants laughed with her. 'The princess has laughed,' they all cried out for joy. She got down, looked more closely and laughed more and more at the capers the people were cutting. The carriage had to turn round and went slowly back to the city beside Gottfried.[23]

We may similarly expect from a fairy tale that Gottfried will now marry the laughing princess and gain power and reputation, and in Bechstein this happens with very few complications (there are rather more in the Grimms' version). But in neither case is the point of this story the happy ending, though that is part of the familiar narrative scheme of the fairy-tale. Nor is it a recognition of the customary fairy-tale dialectic of high and lowly, misery and success. That too would be nothing special. Rather, the particular point of this story lies where the grotesqueness of the action is not diverted into tragedy but is taken up in laughter. For before Gottfried meets his princess there is something tragicomical about the fate of this 'bewitched' woman. At this point all the possibilities of catastrophe are still open. The worst possible outcome is conceivable.

It is the laughter which marks the turning point, the decisive turning point both for the creatures who are stuck and wriggling and for Gottfried and the princess. For the laughter not only bathes this comic scene in the light of reconciliation, so that the trapped people are happily set free. It also brings about a change of heart in the princess and a change of fortune for Gottfried. It is laughter which makes the two of them capable of a relationship. That is especially true for the princess. Now she is in a position to transcend the isolation of her golden cage (the carriage turns round and follows the procession) and relate to her environment. Sorrow had isolated her, laughter revives her. It restores to her the health and humanity that she needs to make her happy, a happiness which, according to the narrative pattern of the story, consists in finding the right partner to marry. Now that means that in laughter this woman's naturalness and humanity returns, so that she is in a position to do the most 'natural' thing in the world: to marry...

Laughter as the power of healing and humanizing. This then emerges not only in folk tales but also in one of the most beautiful literary fairy tales in German literature. The great Swabian poet Eduard Mörike (1804-1875) incorporated it in his 'History of the Beautiful Nymph', a fairy tale about a water nymph who lives in the source of the Danube (the 'Blue Pot') near Ulm. The 'beautiful nymph' lives in the 'Blue Pot', a funnel-shaped whirlpool of great depth which shimmers with blue light. She is not there of her own free will, because she originally came from the Black Sea and is the wife of an 'old Danube sprite' who has banished her into the 'Blue Pot'. Why? Because so far all her children have been stillborn.

That was because she was always sad, without any particular

cause. Her mother-in-law had told her that she would not enjoy a living child until she had laughed heartily five times.[24]

What is exciting about this story is neither its artistic, pseudo-naive, archaizing tone which Mörike imitates brilliantly, nor the neo-mythical scenery which he constructs in narrative form around this indeed enigmatic water. Nor is it that once again the story has a happy ending. What is exciting is the literary strategy by means of which Mörike describes the finding of laughter as a process of humanization. For here, too, sorrow had driven this woman into isolation. Moerover initially she shuns human beings, shuns the light, shuns talking. Only gradually does she come to trust people; only step by step does she relate to them: first to women and children and finally also to a young man. Only step by step does she manage to move towards humanization, towards redeeming, liberating, lifegiving laughter.

The story ends with a picture of the reconciliation between husband and wife. Once he has heard the good news, the 'old Danube sprite' has travelled from the Black Sea to the Blue Pot to take back his wife. This is how she is now described:

> The nymph greeted them from the spring as usual, but now her face was transfigured with joy and her eyes glistened in a way that no one had ever seen before. She said, 'Know that my husband arrived at midnight. My parents-in-law had long since told him that this night I would achieve my good fortune, so he left without delay, with an entourage of princes, his uncle, my brother Synd and many lords. We depart in the morning. The king is as noble and gracious to me as if today I were being his bride for the first time.'[25]

The key words are well placed here. The laughing woman has become the beautiful woman. In other words, laughter is not only therapy for the heart but also beautification for the body. 'You are never more beautiful than when you laugh,' says the man in love to his beloved. And that is precisely what also happens here. Beauty of face matches beauty of soul. Laughter makes people not only healthy but also young and beautiful. It leads to self-renewal, to new birth, to new creation. So it can now be said that 'from today' the husband looks at his wife as though he had never seen her before; looks at her as if he were seeing her for the first time. Thus not only is life given anew to the laughing woman, but she is now in a position to give new life herself: to bear children, to make a new creation possible.

Lost laughter – lost soul: Gottfried Keller

Anyone who laughs is human. If that is the case, so too is the reverse: anyone who can no longer laugh ceases to be human. I would like to demonstrate that from a great story of nineteenth-century German literature: the story of 'The Lost Laugh' which Gottfried Keller (1819-1890) included in his collection *The People of Seldwyla* (Part Two, 1873/74).

This story by the great Swiss narrator is not memorable for the originality of its content. Superficially it is nothing but a love story: its four chapters are about a man and a woman, Jucundus and Justine, who come from the rival villages of Seldwyla and Schwanau. They fall in love, marry, fail, separate and finally rediscover each other. That is nothing particularly original.

What is original is the role of laughter in this text and the combination of individual and social history which makes this novelette a key story for the effects of the modern economic and social revolution in the German-speaking countries at the end of the nineteenth century. By means of his social 'Seldwyla model' Keller shows how the lifestyle which had slipped in since the Middle Ages, based on certain forms of production, was in the process of dissolution and how the harmony not only between social groups and more fundamentally between human beings and nature which had grown up over the centuries was threatening to tip out of balance. Temperament and society are increasingly splitting apart; love is sacrificed to economic calculations; nature (forestry) is increasing treated in terms of its market value; the money economy is becoming abstract (stock markets, shares), and the 'small town' as an independent economic and political unit is increasingly threatened with central control... And because at the end of the twentieth century we can similarly still trace the effects of this economic and social revolution, it is worth recalling a story which tells how it 'all' began.[26]

At three junctures in his story Gottfried Keller has given laughter deep symbolic meaning. First there is the opening scene: Jucundus and Justine get to know each other at a patriotic festival, more precisely a prizegiving at which the Seldwylers are given a victor's garland by one of the most beautiful girls at the festival, Justine. This is what we read at this point:

> All eyes were on her as she got up and took the first garland which had just been awarded to the Seldwylers, to the sound of trumpets and drums. At the same time one could also see Jucundus suddenly standing before her with his banner and laughing in glad happiness. The same beautiful smile shone out from the face of the girl giving the garland like a reflection of his, and it proved that both beings derived from the same homeland from which those gifted with this laugh come.[27]

So here laughter flashes out for the first time in this story. It is important that here laughter is more than a signal of sympathy and trust. Granted, it only flashed out like lightning, yet it can disclose a basic psychological level in both lovers; or more precisely, in a flash it affords both lovers an insight into the homeland from which they come. 'Homeland' here means more than geographical landscape or neighbourhood. Rather, the homeland disclosed in laughter is the inner depth from which the two draw their happiness. In other words, here laughter is an outward expression of the deep inner peace of the soul, an expression of happiness within.

This happiness is not to last. Certainly to begin with the lovers rise above the prejudices and objections of their social environments, marry, and settle in Seldwyla, the husband's home town. Jucundus can even get over the first setbacks in his profession, since with her laughter Justine can once again give his life a positive turn. They move to Schwanau, Justine's home town, to make a new beginning there under what they hope will be more favourable economic and social conditions. Moreover Jucundus has a job in his wife's family's silk-weaving factory.

But it is not long before Jucundus is not only alienated personally from his new environment (his scepticism about religion and his refusal to go to church is a symbol of this), but also has to accept the final failure of his professional plans and business undertakings. This development leads to a breakdown in the couple's marriage, since first Justine feels strongly drawn to religion (in the form of the 'modern' villlage pastor), secondly she detests their economic and social decline in her own village, and thirdly she refuses to follow her husband to a new existence outside it. Here is the decisive passage.

> Passionately and heedlessly and senselessly she shouted that he could go wherever he wanted, but she would not follow him if he could not flourish in her house, where he had lacked nothing and all his wishes were fulfilled. It did not occur to Justine's family or to Justine herself to venture the slightest sacrifice for such a lost life and to throw money after such a person.. From this moment on that attractive and happy laughter disapppeared from the faces of the couple as completely as if it had never been on them.[28]

Anxiety devours the soul: that is the point of this scene. With a keen eye for the social and economic situation of the small-town middle class of his time, Gottfried Keller reflects in his characters the outward and inward failure of men and women in the face of economic pressures in an increasingly complex industrial society based on labour and a modern economy. Significantly Jucundus is portrayed as someone who is too 'slow' and too 'immobile' for new more complicated, more abstract economic processes. He is brutally forced to adapt to harsh economic realities. But he fails, and in the end we have a man who is cheated by his own workers and outplayed by his business rivals, a man of whom it is said: 'A kind of unnatural stupidity attached itself to his soul and veiled his thoughts whenever it was a matter of business, and before six months was up like a hidden marten he had done remarkable damage in the form of a significant loss.'[29]

At this point we have the key word for Jucundus, 'soul', just as in the next section the key word in connection with Justine will be 'anxiety'. For Justine reacts to her husband's failure with nothing but oppressive anger: anger at her family's verdict that she married the wrong man. She is anxious about her loss of 'courage and self-awareness', anxious about poverty, finally anxious that she may lose her church faith, to which she had clung so much at the end... The more anxiety takes over her soul, the more thoroughly laughter disappears. Her lost laughter is matched by her lost 'soul'. And her lost soul is matched by her lost relationship, the couple's alienation, separation and ultimate loneliness. Keller's story shows that without laughter there is no intimacy, no trust, no love. The person who has become incapable of laughing is dead and lost. People who can no longer laugh together are dead to each other.

From this point on the story is told to the end along two lines, but with a symbolic drift. Jucundus, who – outwardly – had reached his nadir but without – inwardly – sacrificing the integrity of his soul (either to the competitive capitalist system or the falsely modernized church system), gradually manages to consolidate his business: he rises socially and politically, but without redis-covering the happiness that he had experienced in his first years with Justine. On the contrary, in the sphere of politics into which he is drawn there is a demon of intrigue, of backbiting, of 'laughing at and doing down', which inwardly utterly repels Jucundus, though outwardly he goes along with it. From now on a sorry earnestness shapes his face as he is confronted with the dilemmas in which he has entangled himself. And this 'earnestness' contrasts with the mob of people, 'laughing and always carousing', who enjoy their life with no concern for the public good. Whereas not the slightest laugh moves his 'sorry face', Jucundus thinks of 'the day on which he had been happy and had innocently enjoyed life'.[30]

But now Jucundus takes a leading position in the sphere of politics and engages in the same intrigues and backbiting as his political opponents. When his supporters resolve to start a new campaign but have no 'ammunition' for it, Jucundus declares himself ready to seek out the 'oil woman', that mysterious woman who takes her nickname 'from the biblical widow with her inexhaustible cruse of oil'. Why? 'Because she no more ran out of good advice and malicious gossip than did the cruse of oil. If you believe that no more rumour or gossip about someone is to be had, this woman, who lives in a remote hut, can still press out a drop of rich oil to slur him with, and she knows how to fill the country with a rumour in a few days.'[31]

It becomes clear that Jucundus's lifeline has split after his separation from his wife. Whereas in the first part, despite his economic decline he had preserved the integrity of his soul, now the reverse is the case: his outward political and social rise is matched by the increasing chilling of his soul. Jucundus sees himself entangled in a web of political relationships from which he can no longer escape unaided, but which further intensify his inner alienation.

With Justine things are precisely the other way round. Her story is told as a story of social decline and the rising liberation of her soul. Justine's family's firm collapses, her reputation in society disappears; she has to earn a living with her own hands. Even the church is no longer a support to her, since the modern pastor who was formerly so admired suddenly gives up his position. Justine is literally confronted with nothingness, spiritually and economically. In her inward and outward distress, on the prompting of an old woman who is travelling through her village on a pilgrimage, she decides to seek out a widow who had once lived with her daughter in Schwanau: Justine thinks that – like the early Christians – this woman has found her happiness in Christian faith. She decides 'to investigate the secret of her peace and her faith'.[32]

The narrative structure is meant to show how the woman who had lost her soul, and thus her laughter, out of anxiety again goes in quest of her soul as a result of the pressure of the crisis in her life. The social conceit, economic success and religious dependence on the church had produced a pseudo-certainty which she could sustain only at the cost of losing her soul. If for Jucundus outward rise is matched by inward alienation, for Justine things are now the other way round: her outward decline is matched by the discovery of her inner self.

In this way the narrator has created a set of circumstances which enables him to arrive at a good ending. For both the former couple are now 'on the way'; both are still unhappy and soulless, though in opposite ways. Now they can meet again, and do so at the home of that 'oil woman' who – as the story now tells us – lives in the same house as the widow whom Justine has sought out. And after both Jucundus rejects the ploys of the 'oil woman' and Justine is repelled by the dryness of the widow's faith, both are ready for a final reconciliation. Keller quite deliberately sets this neither in a private house nor in a political or religious buidling. Rather, the alienation is ended 'beyond' the world of private conceit, of economic competition, political intrigues and church control: in the midst of nature, on one of the beautiful Swiss mountains which Jucundus and Justine make for on the morning of their first reunion. And now it is not surprising that the lost laugh can also return: 'As soon as they turned to each other, the lost laugh returned to their faces, and they embraced and kissed each other warmly.'[33]

But Keller would not have been the great story-teller that he is had he been contented with this simple conclusion 'beyond the world'. For the complex of problems which he has constructed in his story still has to be solved, and a solution must go beyond the private happiness of the lovers. Indeed for Keller laughter stands for more than private peace of the soul and the beauty of a woman who laughs again. And in fact the closing pages of 'The Lost Laugh' also contain pointers towards an economic, political and religious utopia of Gottfried Keller, the writer and the citizen. For while the lovers are wandering arond it is no coincidence that their gaze falls:

1. On a 'beautifully tended plantation'. At this point the plantation symbolizes a form of economy which uses the produce of nature, what Keller saw as a rational economic approach with a concern for the future, since it seemed to be a successful attempt to transform 'the peasant farming economy into a branch of modern industrial production'.[34] Moreover, significantly we are told that this 'plantation' was not created by a landowner but by an 'agricultural association'. It does not just serve to satisfy short-term interests and maximize gain, but has 'a coming century, grandchildren and great-grandchildren' in view. Here Keller is pleading indirectly for an economy based on a collective social contract, caring and responsible towards the future, and not for an economy which is socially antagonistic, heedless and exploitative. Moreover, confronted with this economic option Justinus and Justine can now see 'that the world generally is not as bad as it might be. All these hasty and harsh self-seekers are really taking all this trouble only for their children, and are even fulfilling obligations of welfare for future generations unknown to them!'[35]

But their eye also falls:

2. On a ruined monastery. This is already symbolic enough in itself, since for the two lovers, as for their narrator, the church is a thing of the past. Moreover their new identity, gained in laughter,

no longer needs the comfort of the church. And when asked what one is now to 'make of religion and the church', Jucundus says:

> Nothing... if the Eternal and Infinite is always so silent and hidden, why should not we too for a while quite contentedly and peacefully keep silent? I am tired of the urgency and platitudes of all these uncalled-for people who know nothing and yet keep wanting to pastor me. When the personal figures are withdrawn from a religion, their temples collapse and the rest is silence. But the silence and rest gained is not death but life, which goes on flourishing and shining as on this Sunday morning, and in good conscience we go forward, expectant of things which will or will not come. We go forward in good conscience and undivided; we do not allow head and heart or knowledge and disposition to be torn apart by the well-known wretched commonplaces, since we must go to the judgment which hastens upon everyone as people who are completely undivided in judgment.[36]

That is the final point of this novelette. If economic contradictions can be reconciled, wounds healed, the beauties of nature enjoyed, and the eternal and infinite is not constantly discussed and controlled by uncalled-for people but 'remains silent and hidden', then in the little utopia of this narrative, laughter too can return or, more precisely, in that case laughter in 'The Lost Laugh' is:
• An expression of the 'blossoming beauty' and the 'old happiness' of the lovers;
• An expression of the reconciliation of the soul, the possibility of healing grief and finding one's identity;
• The expression of a socio-economic form of life in a real 'home' – the opposite to heedless selfishness.

Selfishness, a business sense in a negative form – all this spread under the economic conditions of early modern industrial society even among the Swiss middle class. Gottfried Keller already characterized this development with subtle irony in the preface to the second book of his novelettes, *The People of Seldwyla*. The lost laugh is an indicator of a lost identity, a cooling of the soul, a quenching of joy under the pressure of business, in short delivering oneself over to the mercantile spirit and the pursuit of gain:

They are always in motion and come into contact with all the world. They play cards with the most respectable businessmen and are admirably able to give rapid answers to business questions between the hands or to observe a significant silence. In so doing, however, they have already become monosyllabic and dry; they laugh less than before and can find hardly any time to think of pranks and pleasures.[37]

5. Kafka's Laughter

Laughter can be dynamite. Laughter is often incalculable, uncontrollable. Laughing can literally 'seize' people, without any volition or excuse. People can laugh until they shake, double themselves up or get carried away. Laughter has the character of an irrational power. That is probably why laughter knows no limits, no tabus, no moral restraints. One can laugh at everything and, as I have shown, everything is laughed at: the highest and the lowliest, the holiest and the most profane.

Laughing till it hurts: a letter to Felice

None of the great writers of the twentieth century has described the power of laughter as precisely as Franz Kafka of Prague (1883-1924).[38] From 1908 to 1922, as a qualified lawyer Kafka was an employee of the Workers and Accident Assurance Agency for the Kingdom of Bohemia, which was based in Prague. In August 1912 he got to know Felice Bauer, a Jewish woman four years younger than himself. She was later to become Kafka's fiancée, though this did not make his private situation any happier (the engagement was broken off, there was a second engagement and then a final separation in December 1917).

But in September 1912 things had not got that far. That month Kafka made his breakthrough as a writer. In the famous night of 22/23 September he wrote his short story 'The Judgment'. Around four months later, on 8/9 January, he wrote Felice Bauer a letter in which – almost beseechingly – he portrayed himself as a person who could 'also laugh'. Indeed he says that he is even known as a 'great laugher', and as proof he tells the story of something which took place two years previously in his Agency and which had already become a legend in the office. This is what happened.

Kafka and two other colleagues were called before the president of the agency for a promotion, a situation which truly called for dignity and earnestness. Kafka ironically points out that in the eyes of the normal official the meeting with the president was the equivalent of a 'meeting with the Kaiser'. This was still the monarchy at its most formal; Bohemia was still part of Austria, and the old emperor Franz Joseph was still on the throne.

But something must have seemed comic to Kafka about this situation: perhaps it was the 'quintessentially comic status' of this presidential dignitary which had been build up with such gravity; perhaps it was also just an 'uncontrollable mood' at the time. Be this as it may, Kafka was overcome all at once with little outbursts of laughter which he could not stop and did not want to, but which he was able to conceal by artificial coughing. Even the president still noticed nothing, and the ceremony went its way...

Only when the president himself began to speak, 'the usual utterly senseless and platitudinous speech, utterly predictable, nationalistic and delivered in deep solemn tones', could Kafka the employee no longer control himself. He burst out with a laugh which drew everything into its maelstrom:

> First I laughed only at the tiny little jests of the president interspersed here and there. It is the rule that one only smiles gently at such little jokes out of courtesy, but I laughed loudly. I saw my colleagues shaking for fear of infection. I had more sympathy with them than with myself, but I just couldn't help myself, I didn't try to stop it, or put my hand over my mouth. In my helplessness I kept staring the president in the face, incapable of looking away, in all probability sensitively accepting that things couldn't get better but only worse, and that therefore it was best to avoid any change. Of course once I had got going, I no longer laughed just at little jokes as they were made. I laughed at past jokes and future jokes and everything, and no one knew any longer why I was really laughing.[39]

But Kafka was lucky: the reaction of the small gathering to this attack of laughter was first only 'general confusion', no more, especially as the president could not imagine how he himself could be the source and object of this laughter. But as luck would have it, now a colleague of Kafka's began to speak in response to a remark by the president, without noticing that this was the most inappropriate moment both for the president (who was utterly indifferent to everything) and to his poor colleague Franz Kafka, for whom all the barriers against laughter were now down.

So when he started waving his hands about and saying something stupid (in general, and particularly at one point), it all got too much for me. I became completely oblivious to the world, of which previously I had at least been superficially aware, and burst out into that kind of loud heedless laugh of the kind that perhaps only a classroom full of state school children can produce. Silence fell, and now at last I and my laugh were recognized as the focal point. Of course then my knees began knocking with anxiety while I was laughing, and my colleagues could now join in the laughter at will; the coarseness of my laughter, so long prepared and practised, did not strike them and remained comparatively unobserved. Striking my chest with my right hand, partly in recognition of my sin (in recollection of the Day of Atonement) and partly to drive out of my breast all the laughter it contained, I made all kinds of excuses for my laughter, which were perhaps all very convincing but remained totally incomprehensible because of new outbursts of laughter which kept intervening.[40]

But now the president too was disconcerted and Kafka feared the worst. But with his ability to avoid conflicts, the president found some turn of speech and complimented the gentlemen. Kafka himself ends this scene in his letter to Felice with the words: 'Unconquered, with great laughter, but utterly unfortunate, I was the first to stumble from the hall.'

Kafka's laughter – here I shall limit myself to the interpretation of this one autobiographical scene[41] – is remarkable laughter in which the apparently contradictory and completely disparate seem forced together into a paradoxical synthesis. For first Kafka experiences laughter as an ecstatic power over which he no longer has any control, as a point of entry for the irrational, even demonic, which despite all self-discipline evades guidance and domination. Kafka describes precisely how laughter goes beyond the immediate occasion and literally takes over everything. Secondly, Kafka experiences laughter as an endangering of roles which brings about social destabilization. His 'loud reckless laughter' in the presence of a superior threatens to destroy the social role being played out, to put in question the hierarchical relationship between president and deputy and thus jeopardize his own professional existence and that of his colleagues. Kafka lucidly mentions his colleagues' 'fear' of infection and the sympathy that one has with those on the verge of being drawn into the whirlpool of laughter. He also describes lucidly the self-chastisements and gestures of humility (beating the breast), the excuses for so much impertinence. But in vain. His attempt to exorcise the demons of laughter in his own breast is unsuccessful...

Thirdly, Kafka experiences his laughter as something that provokes anxiety, ghastliness and misfortune. There has long ceased to be any trace of joyful, merry, happy laughter. Kafka's laughter is accompanied by knocking knees, trembling at the prospect of discovery, a painful attempt at suppression, by pain in the literal sense. Kafka's laughter is a laughter in which one can double up in agony. The person who laughs becomes almost one possessed, only reflecting afterwards in horror at where laughter has driven him.

Perhaps this explains anxiety about laughter (especially among representatives of any kind of authority). 'Loud, reckless laughter' is seen as a point of entry for the demonic, the diabolical. Those who laugh are seen as fools, doubters, deluded, imprudent, wicked persons who must be compelled to control themselves. Perhaps that explains why representatives of the church in particular have always been concerned to tame, to channel or to functionalize laughter. But the spirit of laughter, once freed, has no intention of going back into the bottle which the moral preachers of every stamp and every century beseechingly hold out to it with cries of ' Come back!'

Laughing at everything? Laughter and ethics

And yet rejection of a humourless moralism does not exempt one from self-critical consideration of a problem which was already posed by Homer and the heedless laughter of the gods; it was not by chance that Plato and Aristotle felt that laughter was a problem that they had to tackle. Certainly one can laugh at everything, and even a prohibition of laughter would be ridiculous. Kafka's laughter in particular shows where such a prohibition would inevitably lead: to laughing cramps, to laughter in which one doubles up in agony...

Yet we still have not settled the question whether one should laugh at everything. Are there (at least for oneself) limits to laughter, self-limitations of which one should be aware, particularly when one is ignoring them? This raises the question of ethical self-commitment, of voluntary self-limitation – precisely because of all the possibilities which laughter offers. There is no question that in many spheres human beings can do more than they should, more than is good for them. For example our technological power is almost boundless, almost uncontrollable. Transferred to the power of laughter this becomes the crucial question, 'Human beings can laugh at anything, but should they?' Henri Bergson was already aware that laughter is 'usually coupled with a certain lack of sensitivity', needs a 'passing anaesthesia of the heart to be able to develop'.[42] But that makes all the more urgent the question, 'Is laughter in principle "beyond good and evil"?'

Someone tells a joke, say about an old man or woman, a handicapped person, a foreigner or a Jew. At first it sounds amusing and provokes laughter. But hardly has the punchline been spoken than one's laughter literally sticks in one's throat: 'Laugh if you can.'[43] One has experienced this countless times, as a witness to ethnic jokes. Such jokes very soon slip over into what one has to call the 'macabre'.

The word 'macabre' is French, and goes back to the biblical story of the Maccabee brothers (told in the books of Maccabees) who willingly accepted a martyr's death for their faith. Therefore 'macabre' always has associations with death (as witness the 'dance macabre') and means something gruesome and dark, horrific and oppressive. Even more, 'macabre' means making jokes about death, illness, and handicap.

The need to refuse to laugh

For Christians whose laughter stems from the spirit of joy and happiness, and who feel particularly committed to the despised and outcast, there are limits to laughter; they have an ethical commitment to refuse to laugh. The writer Dieter Wellershoff has rightly said that jokes in a society can be not only liberating but also repressive, and subject the members of a group to pressure to conform. How often one has experienced people laughing as a result of group pressure, though one would be a spoilsport only to see such laughter as spiteful and humourless. Wellershoff comments: 'Not joining in laughter, often criticized as a sign of being sanctimonious and repressed (which of course can also be the case), is often an unconscious refusal to accept the norms presupposed in the laughter. At times laughter can seem unbearable, the false, intoxicated freedom of a society of philistines.'[44]

So the question of when it is necessary to refuse to laugh also has a dimension which is critical of society. In all highly industrialized countries a socially legitimated entertainment industry has long been established which almost every day is concerned to keep its public in a good mood by making them laugh. The host of gamesmasters, presenters, professional comedians and popular entertainers has become legion. Laughter has deteriorated into the entertainment industry, which in a highly complex information society fulfils its permitted psycho-social function: relaxation, diversion, distracting hearers, viewers or readers from their everyday anxieties. And at the latest the legitimate joking ceases to be funny when it takes on a life of its own and necessary relaxation becomes a narcotic used to distort a critical view of socio-economic contradictions and kills off the drive towards solidarity. In this situation the good joke is purchased at the cost of looking away. 'Having fun' has become a formula used to justify all possible kinds of satisfaction; the threshold of shame which previously made some forms of even perverted sexuality tabu or stigmatized them has been lowered.

Here, too, Fascism in Germany saw to it that the entertainment industry lost its political innocence once and for all. 'Fun', too is a 'master from Germany'. Under this title (a variation of a famous line by Paul Celan, 'Death is a master from Germany'[45]), an impressive documentation has been produced of the way in which the entertainment industry was deliberately exploited and encouraged by the Nazis to divert the people from the brutality of political affairs and especially during the war to keep them in a good mood.[46] 'See to it that the German people learns to laugh again,' Adolf Hitler is said to have remarked; he gave this task to the organizer of the Nazi leisure-time operation 'Power through Joy'. With jokes about Jews, antisemitic ploys, caricatures and not least with the help of entertainment films, the Fascists knew how to use laughter as a drug. A programmed Germany literally laughed itself to death while soldiers were being butchered by the hundred thousand at the front, hundreds of cities were being exterminated in nights of bombing, and millions of Jews were being gassed in the concentration camps. Indeed Jewish jokes had prepared for the pogroms; here too laughter had lowered the threshold of shame and removed the inhibitions which should have been there. That made the work of the executioners all the easier.

So a Christian theology of laughter calls for a modesty about laughter in certain instances, a deliberate refusal to laugh, a protesting objection to laughter. A Christian theology of laughter protests against a laughter above all from above: at the cost of those who in any case are weak, exploited and socially despised; laughter at the expense of human dignity; laughter as a kind of further delimitation and declassification. Such laughter, which has lost any connection with humanity and ethics, is not the expression of a culture of laughter but of an uncultured society in which feelings have grown cold.

Here too the poets have shown the greater sensitivity. In his 1966 *Frankfurt Lectures*, Heinrich Böll pointed out at an early stage that in the history of German culture there have always been two modes of 'humour', only one of which has been really popular. On the one hand there is the mode of Jean Paul (1765-1825), whose work was offered to the Germans as 'resources for an aesthetic of the human'.[47] For Jean Paul's humour in particular was also obligated to the *humanum*. As Böll quotes him: 'Humour as the reversal of the exalted does not annihilate the individual but the finite, by contrasting it with the idea. For humour there is no individual folly, there are no fools, but only foolishness and a mad world.'[48]

In contrast to this there is the humour of Wilhelm Busch (1832-1908), known in Germany above all for his illustrated stories about Max and Moritz (1865). Böll thinks this humour baneful. His reason is this:

Jean Paul could have been chosen: a human being who had humour; but instead the choice was Busch, an inhuman person who illustrated himself. This is the humour of *Schadenfreude*, of malice, and I would not hesitate to describe it as antisemitic, because it is antihuman. It is humour which bets on the contrary laughter of the philistine to whom nothing is holy, nothing, and who is not even intelligent enough to see that in his fearful laughter he is laughing himself to nothing. He is the spirit of decay. For a long time humour has been understood as dragging down from its pillar whatever was exalted, or thought or imagined itself to be exalted. As long as there is still any justification for humour in literature, its humanity could consist in depicting the exaltation of what is dealt with in a derogatory way by society.[49]

Criticism of laughter: the ancients practised it, and when practised against the 'contrary laughter of the philistine to whom nothing is holy', it is still justified today. Moreover this is the point to recall a key passage in the New Testament which also deals with the criticism of laughter and seeks to restore their dignity to all those who are treated 'in a derogatory way' by the dominant society.

Legitimate criticism of laughter: James 4.10

That a theology of laughter which is obligated to the humanity of Jesus goes with a criticism of laughter which is politically and socially relevant is illustrated not only by a saying of Jesus in the New Testament (Luke 6.25), but also by an impressive passage in a relatively late letter, the Letter of James. What is this about?

With almost prophetic weight this letter above all attacks the class opposition between poor and rich. Indeed it contains an explicit theology of poverty: people of lowly status are reminded of their 'exaltation'. God has 'chosen the poor in the world' to make them 'rich' (2.5) through faith. But instead of being respected, the poor are despised by the rich, oppressed, dragged to court and robbed of their dignity (2.6f.) And this by people who have evidently completely suppressed their own 'lowliness' before God. For what is this wealth of the rich? What will happen to them one day? The author replies that 'like the flower of the grass it will pass away. For the sun rises with its scorching heat and withers the grass; its flower falls, and its beauty perishes' (1.10f.).

That is the starting point for the letter of James. The author is obviously addressing a situation of moral decline in or outside the Christian communities, but one which seems to have been completely repressed by the leaders. Blindness in false security is the situation, and people are evidently not yet aware of its moral corruption. How else could the author speak of wars, disputes, the battle of passions, of adulterers and resistance against the devil (4.1-7)? And because the author is evidently dealing with a situation of moral unconcern, libertinism and cheerful heedlessness, he attacks this very point:

> Draw near to God and he will draw near to you. Cleanse your hands, you sinners, and purify your hearts, you men of double mind. Be wretched and mourn and weep. Let your laughter be turned to mourning and your joy to dejection. Humble yourselves before the Lord and he will exalt you (4.8-10).

'Let your laughter be turned to mourning.' It is clear that this statement cannot be exploited for a mediaeval 'theology of tears'. For this is not a sweeping declaration that the state of tears is a state of nearness to God which holds Christians to an attitude of mourning, indeed even artificially produces one. This is a deliberate critique of profligacy and heedlessness which is expressed quite openly in laughter. Here 'laughter' is a symbol of blindness and lack of concern, of self-assurance and social coldness; 'mourning' is a symbol of humility, modesty and social sensitivity.

So in James the criticism of laughter is above all a criticism of moral and social conditions. Anyone who laughs in the way described here has evidently overlooked the misery which prevails everywhere. Such a person feels superior to the poor, even despising them for their poverty. Those who laugh have evidently so far overlooked the social abysses from which they had profited. No wonder, then, that this letter which began with an attack on the rich ends by following up its criticism of laughter with another attack on the rich:

> Come now, you rich, weep and howl for the miseries that are coming upon you. Your riches have rotted and your garments

are moth-eaten. Your gold and silver have rusted, and their rust will be evidence against you and will eat your flesh like fire. You have laid up treasure for the last days. Behold, the wages of the labourers who mow your fields, which you kept back by fraud, cry out; and the cries of the harvesters have reached the ears of the Lord of hosts. You have lived on the earth in luxury, you have fattened your hearts in a day of slaughter. You have condemned, you have killed the righteous man; he does not resist you (5.1-6).

6. Eco's Laughter

However, a Christian theology of laughter will not only plead for a rejection of laughter in particular cases but will also speak out against the absolutizing of laughter, as happens in Umberto Eco's novel, in which a 'postmodern' attitude of 'playing' with all truths is attributed to the mediaeval hero. There is no longer such a thing as the truth about God, and an attitude of irony, parody and laughter about everything under the sun has taken its place. At the end of this essay – as I indicated – I want to take up the challenge of Eco's novel, reflect on its consequences and develop a theological alternative.

Against making the question of God a matter of indifference

Both the basic philosophical statements and the action of the novel, inside and outside its framework, have so far as a rule been played down by theological critics. For example the Brazilian liberation theologian Leonardo Boff in his reflections on Eco's novel points only to the 'relativizing and liberating function of laughter'. He does not take its basic antimetaphysical option into account. William of Baskerville's scepticism about the truth ('Perhaps in the end there is only one thing to do if one loves people, namely to make them laugh about the truth') is trivialized by Boff into an ethic of love: 'Everything depends on whether one loves real people or formulas, formal truths. If we really love people, we discover that they are infinitely more complex than any truth, that their life is worth more than all truths, that we are nothing before God and that all that we are comes from God as a gift to be enjoyed happily.'[50]

Such a reading of the novel in terms of an ethic of love has failed to understand the radical challenge I discussed in the first part of this essay as much as a historicizing account fails to understand it. Certainly we can follow the theologian Michael Thomas[51] in recognizing in the positions of William and Adso traditions of mediaeval philosophy (nominalism along the line of William of Ockham) and German mysticism (Meister Eckhardt and Angelus Silesius). Indeed William – just like Ockham – refers to the 'free will of God' which cannot be recognized by human beings with the help of reason. And Adso's talk of God as 'sheer nothingness' is a direct quotation from Meister Eckhart. But all this is unmistakably exploited for a problematization of truth which makes the question of God a matter of indifference, basic scepticism as to whether or not God really exists. That is more early Wittgenstein than Ockham, more postmodern semiotics than mediaeval mysticism.

So the Tübingen theologian and philosopher Georg Wieland has quite rightly stressed the decisive difference between the fictitious William of Baskerville and the real William of Ockham which is central to the interpretation of the basic philosophical stratum of the novel. Certainly Ockham and Eco are at one over the theory of signs: 'As the world is nothing but the sum of all the individual things in the world, the knowledge of the world also changes. It no longer understands the world as the realization of an order underlying it, and thus is not longer essentially the limitation of order, but increasingly becomes a creative process through which individual things are ordered so that they become a meaningful whole.'[52] But at the same time – according to Wieland – the mediaeval philosopher and theologian has nothing to do with the 'renunciation of truth' and the 'silence' about God intended in the novel.

In fact we have to see that behind the positions of William and Adso in this novel there is ultimately an indifference to the question of God. Here too Wieland has seen the decisive point: 'If one increasingly makes the God-world relationship something of which human beings have no clear idea – and this is precisely what happens through the centring of theological reflection on the divine perspectives of omnipotence and freedom – then the point is soon reached when whether or not there is a God becomes a question which makes no difference to action in this world. William's thought seems to me to be moving along this line. This hypothesis is confirmed by his proposal for therapy: he does not recommend any traditionalist or reformist renewal of the *status quo*, nor does he stress the liberating effect of truth, but rather the human effect of laughter.'[53] And as we have also seen, this laughter is 'something like the last means of human self-assertion against institutions which despise human beings'.[54]

Against the mad alternative

So as a theologian one will hesitate simply to adopt William's position on laughter, liberating though it may seem in the face of the criminal fanaticism about the truth represented by Jorge de Burgos, and beneficent though it may seem in comparison with the Inquisitor's terrorism on behalf of the truth. Nevertheless, we will do better not to rely on the fact that laughter 'at' the truth really makes people free. For to laugh at the truth is no way to freedom. On the contrary, it is a way into the realm of the labyrinth, the arbitrary, the inscrutable – both metaphysically and ethically. Such a laugh – though it may seem free in comparison with a church relying on power – does not really lead to freedom but to resignation, because while the contradictions in church and society may be being laughed at, they cannot be laughed away.

So it is no coincidence that at the end of his life Adso can believe neither in the God of glory nor in the God of joy nor in the God of mercy. A liberating, messianic laugh as a sign of the new beginning, the new life, trust in creation and the Creator, cannot be found either in William or in Adso. Remarkably, one finds no trace of a discipleship of Christ and a Pauline dialectic of life in these Christian monks, which again proves that they have sprung less from a Christian than from a 'postmodern' spirit.

The picture of the church in this novel is similar. The church is not experienced here as a community of people freed by Christ for freedom, but as the sphere of a mad alternative: a fanatical apocalyptic mania for destruction (Jorge) and the terrorism of the Inquisition in support of the truth (Bernardo Gui) on the one hand, and mystical inwardness (Adso) and spiritual individualism

(William) on the other. Here we have the church only as a place either for demonstrating the power of inquisitors and apocalyptists or as a sphere of private withdrawal by a spiritual elite.[55]

There is no sign here of a third way, a third form of the church lived out as a community of disciples of Christ. This could emerge only if one entertains the possibility of a theology of laughter which does not play God off against laughter either by sceptically mocking all truth (William) or denouncing it as a gateway by which the devil can enter the church (Jorge). This will be a theology of laughter which has its deepest source in a God who can join in laughter with his creatures and despite everything has more 'joy' in the sinner who repents than in the mass of just people who think that they need no repentance; a theology of laughter which is aware of the two sides of which I have spoken; a theology of laughter as a form of reconciled co-existence with the contradictions of the world without suppressing them or allowing itself to be forced by them into fatalistic resignation.

So in the face of the mad alternative that has just been described, it is no coincidence that in the case of a monk like Adso of Melk the last word is not a wish for fulfilment and consummation by God but the longing for extermination, for immersion 'in the desolate and barren deity'. This 'deity' of his is evidently as 'desolate and barren' as the world itself, whose signs have not been understood and which must now seem like a dance of death, a ship of fools, because everything rests on 'chance' and no 'message' can be recognized anywhere. And however much this basic experience of the fictitious monk in Eco's novel is also the basic experience of countless contemporaries of the twentieth century, Christian theology will do well to argue patiently against it.

Against 'postmodern' aestheticism

In the first part of this book I attempted to show that Eco's understanding of science ('semiotics') and aesthetics ('irony, meta-linguistic play, enunciation squared') corresponds to the spirit of 'postmodernity' in the third sense that I described: the 'signs' of reality never completely comprehend it; rather, reality is constituted by sign systems which have many references, the meaning of which can never fully be grasped. These basic philosophical premises can be demonstrated most vividly in the sphere of aesthetics, for example in the novel. Therefore Eco's *Name of the Rose* is not to be understood as a continuation of his philosophical and linguistic works by means of fiction. The literary critic and theologian Hermann Kelber has hit the point here: 'The historical novel and the detective story are particularly appropriate for making clear what Eco wanted to express. Both forms of novel propagate a "world order" and a correspondence between the order of thought and the order of the world in a special way. But because they are fictitious, because they are *a priori* understood as fiction, the reader does not think of regarding the fictitious orders as real.'[56]

So it is fully in accord with Eco's strategy of breaking up monopolies of truth that he should encipher his 'postmodern' messages in a work of art. In this way they remain aesthetic formations, artistic products which represent only what Eco thinks of reality generally: it can be interpreted in many ways, has many references, is as confusing as a labyrinth. The only truths which are any use are simply instruments which one can throw away after using them, since the totality in any case remains impenetrable.

However, it is impossible for the believer, the Christian, to remain permanently in the aesthetic sphere, however much he or she may admire the artificial refinement of a work of art. What is allowed the artist is not permissible for the believer: to leave decisions open, to replay the game *ad infinitum*, to keep exchanging the masks and roles for new ones and continually enjoying the expression of a 'postmodern' aesthetics: 'Irony, metalinguistic play, enunciation squared'. Rather, believers feel challenged to a basic decision about their life and death, an ultimate seriousness and an infinite wager: discipleship of Christ and thus trust in the God who has shown himself in Jesus Christ. All aesthetic play stops when the answer must be yes or no. All irony comes to an end when a decision is required. All masquerade is over when everything is in earnest. In this sense Hermann Kelber is right in his criticism of Eco's novel: 'Eco's *The Name of the Rose* as an aesthetic plan is a postmodern myth, a renewed symbiosis of poetical and metaphysical thought. However, in this postmodern myth everything remains optional, without any metaphysical weight or moral obligation.'[57]

Laughter means that the facts of the world are not the end of the matter

And because the believer is really serious about making a decision, it is worth recalling the case of the philosopher Ludwig Wittgenstein, whose remark about the 'ladder' in the *Tractatus* was given to William of Baskerville. For if we look closely, the fictitious Franciscan in Eco's novel gives Wittgenstein's original statement the opposite meaning. For William, the ladder of the knowledge of reality is 'useful' but ultimately 'meaningless'. William is being consistent, since he has not succeeded in discovering a 'meaning' in all these signs. His trust in a total meaning is destroyed. But for Wittgenstein himself it is precisely the other way round: the ladders can be thrown away because the knower can see the world 'rightly' after using them. Moreover Ludwig Wittgenstein's *Tractatus* ultimately has a constructive purpose, for all its critical and destructive tendency. To some degree it represents merely the negative side of Wittgenstein's attempts to conceive of something like a world of transcendence and metaphysics under the conditions of the twentieth century. Already in the *Tractatus* we find sentences like this: 'The sense of the world must lie outside the world. In the world everything is as it is and happens as it does happen. *In* it there is no value – and if there were, it would be of no value.'[58]

But Wittgenstein entrusted his real concern to his *Notebooks*. On 11 July 1916 we find the following entry in them:

What do I know about God and the purpose of life?
I know that this world exists.
That I am placed in it like my eye in its visual field.
That something about it is problematic, which we call its
     meaning.
That this meaning does not lie in it but outside it.
That life is the world.
That my will penetrates the world.
That my will is good or evil.

Therefore that good and evil are somehow connected with the
   meaning of the world.
The meaning of life, i.e. the meaning of the world, we can call
   God
and connect with this the comparison of God to a father.
To pray is to think about the meaning of life.[59]

Or even more clearly in a subsequent passage: 'To believe in a
God means to see that the facts of the world are not the end of
the matter. To believe in God means to see that life has a meaning.'[60]

So a theology of laughter can certainly refer to Wittgenstein in
its basic 'metaphysical' assumptions. Christians who laugh are
expressing their feeling that the facts of the world are not the end
of the matter, though this world need not be despised. Christians
who laugh are taking part in God's laughter at his creation
and his creatures, and this laughter is a laughter of mercy and
friendliness. Christians who laugh are expressing resistance to a
'postmodern' ideology in which everything is optional, to an
aesthetic of indifference, and to a fanatical mania about the truth
and the use of violent terrorism to defend the truth. Christians
who laugh are insisting that the stories of the world's sufferings
do not have the last word, and are also offering sufficient
opportunity to penetrate an attitude of 'postmodern optionalism'
and an aesthetics of irony and enunciation and to show solidarity
with those who have nothing to laugh about in this world.
   Here one might call to mind a remark by the American
theologian Harvey Cox from his book *Feast of Fools*, a book
from which I have already quoted and which is still worth reading:
'Laughter is hope's last weapon. Crowded on all sides with idiocy
and ugliness, pushed to concede that the final apocalypse seems
to be upon us, we seem nonetheless to nourish laughter as our
only remaining defence. In the presence of disaster and death we
laugh instead of crossing ourselves. Or perhaps better stated, our
laughter is our way of crossing ourselves. It shows that despite
the disappearance of any empirical basis for hope, we have
not stopped hoping...It could conceivably disappear, and where
laughter and hope have disappeared, man has ceased to be man.'[61]

Notes and Bibliography

Mottos, Preface and Introduction

1. John Chrysostom, *St Chrysostom: Homilies on the Gospel of Matthew*, Post-Nicene Christian Library, New York 1888, Homily VI.9, p.41.
2. J.W.von Goethe, *Faust*, Prologue in Heaven, vv. 275-8.
3. I.Kant, *Kritik of Judgment*, translated by J.H.Bernard, London 1892, Part I, I. 54. I owe this quotation to Hans Küng, who used it as a motto for his sixty-fifth birthday celebrations on 19 March 1993.
4. M.Frank, 'Über Komik, Witz und Ironie. Überlegungen im Ausgang von der Frühromantik', in T.Vogel (ed.), *Vom Lachen. Einem Phänomen auf der Spur*, Tübingen 1992, 211.
5. Vogel (ed.), *Vom Lachen* (see n.4).
6. H.Heine, 'Ein Weib', in *Sämtliche Schriften*, ed. K.Briegleb, Vol.VII (1837–1844), Munich 1976, 374.
7. H.Bergson, *Laughter*, London 1911, 200.
8. It has proved impossible to produce a generally valid definition of what is comic and laughable. Instead, the insight has become established that what is comic differs widely, depending on the producer and the situation, and on the historical and cultural context. No single theory is adequate any longer here. According to Aristotle, one laughs because one sees a defect in a person associated with ugliness. For Plato, one laughs if one perceives a discrepancy between being and appearance in other people. For Thomas Hobbes, one laughs if one feels superior to other people (the incongruity or contrast theory of the comic, *On Human Nature*, 1650). According to Kant, one laughs if a tense expectation suddenly dissolves into nothingness ('theory of the breakthrough of expectation', *Critique of Judgment*, 54). According to Bergson one laughs at the unadapted, alien, narrow person, at his or her automatism and mechanical way of doing things, so that this mode of behaviour is subject to social sanction (*Laughter*, 1911). But the comic can also be defined as an experience of discrepancy and disproportion ('contrast theory', thus e.g. H.Plessner, 'Lachen und Weinen. Eine Untersuchung der Grenzen menschlichen Verhaltens', *Gesammelte Schriften* VII, Frankfurt am Main 1982, 201-387), or in the framework of a functionally orientated analysis of a situation as social provocation

(the theory of 'rule violation', thus e.g. J.Ritter, 'Über das Lachen', in id., *Subjektivität*, Frankfurt am Main 1974, 62-92). There is abundant material on the theories of the comic in W.Preisendanz and R.Warning (eds.), *Das Komische*, Poetik und Hermeneutik VII, Munich 1976. Also recently B. Greiner, *Die Komödie. Eine theatralische Sendung: Grundlagen und Interpretationen*, Tübingen 1992 (esp. Chapter I, 'Komiktheorien').

9. I need refer only to the book by G.Heinz-Mohr, *Der lachende Christ. Geistlicher Humor quer durch Deutschland*, Freiburg 1988. The books by G.Kranz, *Das göttliche Lachen*, Würzburg 1970, and H.Thielecke, *Das Lachen der Heiligen und Narren. Nachdenkliches über Witz und Humor*, Freiburg 1975, are more profound.

10. H.Lenk, *Kritik der kleinen Vernunft. Einführung in die jokologische Philosophie*, Frankfurt am Main 1987, paperback 1990.

I Problems with Laughter – A Philosophical and Theological Tableau

1. I have quoted from *The Iliad of Homer*, translated by Richmond Lattimore, Chicago 1951, reissued New York 1991.

2. For the phenomenon of the 'laughter of the gods', cf. K.Kerényi, *Antike Religion*, Wiesbaden 1971, 137-46; L.Golden, 'Geloion in the "Iliad"', *Harvard Studies in Classical Philology* 93, 1990, 47-57; S.Halliwell, 'The Uses of Laughter in Greek Culture', *The Classical Quarterly* 85, NS 41, 1991, 279-96; R.Muth, *Die Götterburleske in der griechischen Literatur*, Darmstadt 1992.

3. In his survey of current theories of the comic, the literary critic Hans Robert Jauss distinguishes 'two basically different aspects' in the comic, 'depending on whether the comic arises from the demotion of a heroic ideal to a counter-worldliness or whether it originates from the promotion of the material physicality of huamn nature': H.R.Jauss, 'Über den Grund des Vergnügens am komischen Helden', in W.Preisendanz and R.Waring (ed.), *Das Komische*, Munich 1976, 104.

4. Muth, *Die Götterburleske* (n.2), 22.

5. Thus rightly B.Greiner, 'Das "Homerische Gelächter"', in id., *Die Komödie. Eine theatrische Sendung. Grundlagen und Interpretationen*, Tübingen 1992, 18-24: 20.

6. Quotations are from *The Odyssey of Homer*, translated by Richmond Lattimore, Chicago 1965, reissued New York 1991. Scholars still dispute whether or not Homer was the author of the *Odyssey*, so I cautiously put the word 'Homer' in quotation marks in this case.

7. There is a discussion in Greiner, *Die Komödie* (n.5), 18-42.

8. Muth, *Die Götterburleske* (n.2), 20.

9. Ibid.

10. P.Friedländer, 'Lachende Götter', in *Die Antike. Zeitschrift für Kunst*

und Kultur des klassischen Altertums, ed. W.Jaeger, X, Berlin and Leipzig 1934, 209-26: 217.

11. Ibid.
12. Both quotations are from Hesiod, *Works and Days*, 52-9, in *Hesiod and Theognis*, translated by D.Wender, Harmondsworth 1973.
13. Cf.Muth, *Die Götterburleske* (n.2), 22.
14. Especially in his comedy *The Birds*. Cf. now Greiner, *Die Komödie* (n.5), 32-46.
15. M.Mader, *Das Problem des Lachens und der Komödie bei Platon*, Stuttgart, Berlin, Cologne and Mainz 1977, 80.
16. H.-G.Gadamer, 'Platos dialektischer Ethik. Phänomenologische Interpretationen zum Philebos' (1931), in id., *Platons dialektische Ethik und andere Studien zur platonischen Philosophie*, Hamburg 1968, 148-51.
17. Mader, *Das Problem des Lachens* (n.15), 25. For the interpretation of laughter in behavioural research cf. I.Eibl-Eibesfeldt, *Grundriss der vergleichenden Verhaltensforschung*, Munich ³1972.
18. Mader, *Das Problem des Lachens* (n.15), 23.
19. Cf. Plato, *Laws*, 732c, 735.
20. Plato, *Thaeatetus*, 174ab, translation from B.Jowett (ed.), *The Dialogues of Plato* III, Oxford ³1892, 232.
21. H.Blumenberg, *Das Lachen der Thrakerin. Eine Urgeschichte der Theorie*, Frankfurt am Main 1987.
22. Cf.Plato, *Thaeatetus*, 174c-175a.
23. M.Führmann, *Die Dichtungstheorie der Antike. Eine Einführung*, Darmstadt ²1992, 85. Cf. also E.Grassi, *Die Theorie des Schönen in der Antike*, Cologne 1962, new edition Cologne 1982, esp.108-40. For Plato's attitude to the poets see also H.G.Gadamer, 'Platon und die Dichter' (1934), in id., *Platons dialektische Ethik und andere Studien zur platonischen Philosophie*. Hamburg 1968, 181-204.
24. Plato, *Republic*, X.4, from Jowett, *Dialogues* (n.20), 601.
25. Ibid., Jowett, 602.
26. Plato, *Republic*, III.3.
27. Plato, *Republic*, II.21.
28. Aristotle, 'Parts of Animals', III.10, tr. E.S.Forster, Loeb Classical Library, London and Cambridge, Mass. 1937.
29. F.Nietzsche, 'Aus dem Nachlass der Achtzigerjahre', in *Werke*, ed. K.Schlechta, Munich 1966, III, 467.
30. Aristotle, *Nicomachean Ethics*, IV.4, from W.D.Ross (ed. and trans.), *Works of Aristotle*, Oxford 1925.
31. Ibid.
32. Ibid.
33. Aristotle, *Rhetoric*, XVIII.7, Loeb Classical Library, ed. J.H.Freese, London and Cambridge, Mass. 1926.
34. Ibid.
35. Führmann, *Die Dichtungstheorie der Antike* (n.23), 75.

36. This and the previous quotation are from Aristotle, *On the Art of Poetry*, translated by Ingram Bywater, ch.2, ch.5.

37. Ibid., ch.6.

38. Ibid.

39. U.Eco, *The Name of the Rose*, London and New York 1980. For Eco's novel see U.Eco, *Reflections on The Name of the Rose*, London and New York 1985; A.Haverkam and A.Heit (eds.), *Ecos Rosenroman. Ein Kolloquium*, Munich 1987; also G.Kroeber (ed.), *Zeichen im Umberto Ecos Roman 'Der Name der Rose'*, Munich 1987; T.Stauder, *Umberto Ecos 'Der Name der Rose'. Forschungsbericht und Interpretation. Mit einer kommentierten Bibliographie der ersten sechs Jahre internationaler Kritik (1980-1986)*, Erlangen 1988 (for laughter see above all 71-5). Eco has commented on the theory of laughter in connection with Pirandello: U.Eco, 'Pirandello ridens', in id., *The Limits of Interpretation*, Bloomington, Indiana 1990,. 163-73.

40. Eco, *The Name of the Rose*, 77.

41. Ibid., 79.

42. Ibid., 81.

43. Ibid., 95.

44. For Thomas Aquinas cf. U.Eco, 'In Praise of Thomas Aquinas', in id., *Travels in Hyperreality*, New York 1986, 257-68. See also the extremely informative 'Aesthetics of the Middle Ages', in U.Eco, *Art and Beauty in the Middle Ages*, New Haven 1986.

45. Eco, *The Name of the Rose*, 130.

46. Ibid., 131.

47. Ibid.

48. Ibid., 132.

49. Ibid., 468.

50. Ibid., 472.

51. Ibid., 474ff.

52. For the discussion of postmodernity cf. H.Küng, *Global Responsibility*, London and New York 1991, 19-24; also D.R.Griffin, *God and Religion in the Postmodern World. Essays in Postmodern Theology*, Albany, New York 1989. M.Schnell is at present preparing a dissertation at the Institute for Ecumenical Research on the reception of postmodernity in contemporary theology.

53. J.Habermas, *Der Philosophische Diskurs der Moderne. Zwölf Vorlesungen*, Frankfurt am Main 1985: J.B.Metz, *Zukunftsfähigkeit. Suchbewegungen im Christentum*, Freiburg 1987 (with F.-X.Kaufmann).

54. J.B.Metz, 'Gotteskrise. Ein Portrait des zeitgenössischen Christentums', *Süddeutsche Zeitung*, 24/25 June 1993.

55. R.Barthes, *Criticism and Truth*, London 1987; id., *The Pleasure of the Text*, London 1976; id., *S/Z*, London 1975; J.F.Lyotard, *The Postmodern Condition*, Manchester 1984.

56. L.Fiedler, *Collected Essays*, New York 1971. There is a good survey of

the discussion in A.Huyssen and K.R.Scherpe (eds.), *Postmoderne. Zeichen eine kulturellen Wandels*, Hamburg 1986.

57. U.Eco, *A Theory of Semiotics*, London 1976, 6.
58. U.Eco, 'Postmodernism, Irony and Contentment', in id, *Reflections on the Name of the Rose* (n.39), 66.
59. Ibid., 66f.
60. Ibid., 67, 68.
61. T. de Lauretis, 'Das Rätsel der Lösung – Umberto Ecos "Name der Rose" als postmoderner Roman', in A.Huyssen and K.R.Scherpe (eds.), *Postmoderne* (n.56), 251-69: 255f.
62. G.Seibt, 'Heilige Zeichen. Der Erzähler und die Wissenschaft vom Lügen: Umberto Eco wird 60', *Frankfurter Allgemeine Zeitung*, 4 January 1992. The allusion to the 'penny dreadful' relates to Eco's second great novel, *Foucault's Pendulum*, London and New York 1989. For Eco's own work on semiotics see also U.Eco, *Semiotics and the Philosophy of Language*, London and Bloomington 1984. One of his early works still remains basic for his own poetics: U.Eco, *Opera aperta*, Milan 1962.
63. T.de Lauretis has rightly remarked in her article: 'It is only consistent that in his later works Eco should put forward the theory that semiotics is "a theory of lies" and that the human being is the only animal that can lie and laugh. Understood in this way a text is always a lie, often a deliberate lie, and its greatest power is laughter. Long before Eco wrote the novel which deals with the quest for the mysterious Urtext on comedy, the text about the truth of laughter, he had written about de Amici's popular pamphlet *Cuore*: "Either one laughs about the [civil] order or one must curse it from outside; either one acts as though one accepts it in order then to be able to show it up, or one acts as though one rejects it, in order then to reintroduce it in another form; either one is Rabelais or Descartes." In *The Name of the Rose*, I think Eco wants to do both' (253f.). Cf. also P.V.Zima, in id., *Literarische Ästhetik. Methoden und Modelle der Literaturwissenschaft*, Tübingen 1991, 282-95.
64. Eco, *The Name of the Rose*, 491.
65. Ibid., 492.
66. Ibid.
67. L.Wittgenstein, *Tractatus Logico-philosophicus*, London 1922, nos.6.54 and 7, p. 189.
68. Eco, *The Name of the Rose*, 492.
69. Ibid., 493.
70. Ibid.
71. Ibid.
72. Ibid.
73. Ibid., 501.
74. Ibid.

75. Eco, *Postscript* (n.39), 33f.
76. In his *Postscript* Eco has described precisely the kind of labyrinth he was thinking of: 'And finally there is the net, or rather rhizome. The rhizome is so constructed that every path can be connected with every other one. It has no centre, no periphery, no exit, because it is potentially infinite. The space of conjecture is a rhizome space. The labyrinth of my library is still a mannerist labyrinth, but the world in which William realizes he is living already has a rhizome structure; that is, it can be structured but is never structured definitively' (57f.).
77. See Part IV.6 below.

II Human Laughter and God's Laughter – A Biblical Tableau

1. M.Bakhtin, *Literatur und Karneval. Romantheorie und Lachkultur* (1965), Munich 1969.
2. Cf. the criticism by D.R.Moser, 'Lachkultur des Mittelalters? Michael Bachtin und die Folgen seiner Theorie', *Euphorion. Zeitschrift für Literaturgeschichte* 84, 1990, 89-111.
3. Thus H.Bausinger, 'Lachkultur', in Vogel (ed.), *Vom Lachen*, 9-22: 15 (see Ch.1 n.4).
4. Sources are given for this quotation and the other texts in this and the next section in G.Schmitz, 'Ein Narr, der da lacht... Überlegungen zu einer mittelalterlichen Verhaltensnorm', in Vogel, *Vom Lachen* (ch.I, n.4); id., '*quod rident homines, plorandum est*. Der Unwert des Lachens in monastisch geprägten Vorstellungen der Spätantike und des frühen Mittelalters', in *Stadtverfassung – Verfassungsstaat – Pressepolitik. FS für E.Naujoks zum 65. Geburtstag*, ed. F.Quarthal and J.W.Sekler, Sigmaringen 1980, 31-5.
5. Jerome, *Tractatus in Psalmos* LXXXIII, CCL 78, 1958, pp.99, 125-9.
6. Augustine, *Sermo* 31, Migne PL 38, 194: '*et rident homines, et plorant homines; et quod rident homines, plorandum est.*'
7. Chrysostom, *St Chrysostom: Homilies on the Gospel of Matthew*, Post-Nicene Christian Library, New York 1888, Homily VI.5.
8. Ibid., 6.
9. E.R.Curtius, *Europäische Literatur und lateinisches Mittelalter*, Bern 1948, 423f.: 423.
10. Schmitz, 'Ein Narr, der da lacht...' (n.4), 132f.
11. I am following the proposal by the Münster Catholic Old Testament scholar E.Zenger, *Das Erste Testament. Die jüdische Bibel und die Christen*, Düsseldorf 1991.
12. J.Ebach, ' "Nein, du hast doch gelacht." Annäherung an eine biblische Wundergeschichte – zugleich: eine weitere Ecce-homo-Variation', *Einwürfe* IV, Munich 1987, 56-78: 76, 77.
13. D.Arenhoevel, *Erinnerung an die Väter. Genesis 12-50*, Stuttgart 1976, 71.

14. Ebach, ' "Nein, du hast doch gelacht" ' (n.12), 78.
15. W.Gross, *Glaubensgehorsam als Wagnis der Freiheit. Wir sind Abraham*, Mainz 1980, 36.
16. For the history of the dispute over the interpretation of this psalm see H.Schreiner (ed.), *Beiträge zur Psalmforschung. Psalm 2 und 22*, Würzburg 1988. That the 'Sitz im Leben' of this psalm is the oppressed post-exilic community has recently been stressed above all by E.Zenger, *Mit meinem Gott überspringe ich Mauern. Einführung in das Psalmenbuch*, Freiburg im Breisgau 1987, 47-52.
17. Thus H.-J.Kraus, *Psalms 1-69*, Minneapolis 1993, *ad loc.*
18. F.Nietzsche, *Beyond Good and Evil*, translated by Helen Zimmern, London 1909, no .294; cf. T.Kunnas, *Nietzsches Lachen. Eine Studie über das Komische im Nietzsches Werken*, Munich 1982.
19. For this problem see W.Gross and K.J.Kuschel, *'Ich schaffe Finsternis und Unheil!'. Ist Gott verantwortlich für das Übel?*, Mainz 1992.
20. That has been clearly demonstrated by the dissertation written by my colleague G.Langenhorst, *Hiob unser Zeitgenosse. Die literarische Rezeption der biblischen Figur im 20. Jahrhundert als theologische Herausforderung* (in preparation, Mainz 1994).

III *The Laughter of Christians: New Testament Foundations*

1. 'The Coptic gnostic Apocalypse of Peter', in W.Schneemelcher (ed.), *New Testament Apocrypha* II, Louisville and Cambridge 1992, 705-9: 708. For the dating and theological self-understanding of the work see the introduction by A.Werner.
2. The essentials of christology can be found in K.-J.Kuschel (ed.), *Born Before All Time? The Dispute over Christ's Origin*, London and New York 1992. K.Rudolph, *Gnosis*, Edinburgh 1984, reissued New York 1987, is a basic introduction. For the philosophical significance of Gnosticism see recently P.Sloterdijk and T.Macho (eds.), *Weltrevolution der Seele. Ein Lese- und Arbeitsbuch der Gnosis von der Spätantike bis zur Gegenwart* (two vols.), Munich 1991.
3. Irenaeus, *Against the Heresies*, I.24.4.
4. 'The Second Doctrine of the Great Seth', in J.M.Robinson (ed.), *The Nag Hammadi Library in English*, New York 1977, 332.
5. Cf. the introduction by J.Dart, *The Laughing Saviour. The Discovery and Significance of the Nag Hammadi Gnostic Library*, New York 1976.
6. Thus O.Betz, *Der Humor und die Fröhlichkeit der Christen*, Ulm ²1982; W.Thiede, *Das verheissene Lachen. Humor in theologischer Perspektive*, Göttingen 1986. The study by the American exegete E.Trueblood, *The Humor of Christ*, New York 1964, is no better. L.Kretz, *Witz, Humor und Ironie bei Jesus*, Olten and Freiburg im Breisgau 1981; id., *Der Reiz des Paradoxen bei Jesus*, Olten and Freiburg im Breisgau 1983, are more

convincing; cf. also *Bibel heute* 28, 1992, thematic volume *Nie soll er gelacht haben? Spuren des Humors Jesu.*

7. 'Protevangelium of James', in Schneemelcher (ed.), *New Testament Apocrypha* I, Louisville and Cambridge 1991, 236-37: 433.

8. Thus E.Norden, *Die Geburt des Kindes. Geschichte einer religiösen Idee* (1924), Darmstadt 1969, 67 (Ch.4, 'Das lachende Sonnenkind und der himmlische Bräutigam'). Cf. also P.Schwarzenau, *Das göttliche Kind. Der Mythos vom Neubeginn*, Stuttgart 1984, ²1988.

9. 'Pseudo Gospel of Matthew', in Schneemelcher (ed.), *New Testament Apocrypha* I (n.7), 462.

10. Norden, *Die Geburt des Kindes* (n.8), 66.

11. Quoted in W.Guglielmi, 'Das Lachen der Götter und Menschen am Nil. Die religiöse und alltagsweltliche Bedeutung des Lachens im Alten Ägypten', in Vogel (ed.), *Vom Lachen* (I n.4), 154-73: 156.

12. W.Haug, 'Das Komische und das Heilige. Zur Komik in der religiösen Literatur des Mittelalters', in id., *Strukturen als Schlüssel zur Welt. Kleine Schriften zur Erzählliteratur des Mittelalters*, Tübingen 1989, 349-61: 356.

13. 'Infancy Gospel of Thomas', in W.Schneemelcher (ed.), *New Testament Apocrypha* I, 444-9:446.

14. P.Sloterdijk, *Kritik der zynischen Vernunft*, Frankfurt am Main 1983, I, 305f.

15. Here Kretz, *Witz, Humor und Ironie bei Jesus* (n.6), offers a wealth of material. The analysis in this study by Kretz is particularly convincing. But its title is misleading: it is not in fact an analysis of Jesus' wit, humour and irony but a demonstration of grotesque images, bold similes, disarming replies, paradoxes and perplexing exclamations of happiness.

16. In this case I am following the convincing translation by W.Jens, *Und ein Gebot ging aus. Das Lukas-Evangelium*, Stuttgart 1991, 40.

17. A.Brandstetter, 'Bibel und Humor', in J.Holzner and U.Zeilinger (eds.), *Die Bibel im Verständnis der Gegenwartsliteratur*, St Pölten and Vienna 1988, 99-108: 100f.

18. Thus in the resolution of the Joint Synod of Dioceses in the Federal Republic of Germany, 'Unsere Hoffnung', in *Offizielle Gesamtausgabe* I, Freiburg im Breisgau 1976, 104.

19. For this whole problem see R.L.Wilken, *The Christians as the Romans Saw Them*, New Haven 1984.

20. H.Cox, *The Feast of Fools*, Cambridge, Mass. 1969, 140f.

21. Cf. K.-J.Kuschel, *Jesus in der deutschsprachigen Gegenwartsliteratur*, Gütersloh and Zurich 1978, paperback Munich 1987. See the references to or interpretations of G.Hauptmann and H.Böll.

22. H.Heine, 'Deutschland. Ein Wintermärchen', in *Sämtliche Schriften*, ed. K.Briegleb, Munich 1976, VII, 605. For Heine see K.-J.Kuschel, *'Vielleicht hält Gott sich einige Dichter.' Literarisch-theologische Por-*

traits, Mainz 1991 (Ch.II, 'Heinrich Heine und die Doppelgesichtigkeit aller Religion').

23. M.C.Jacobelli, *Ostergelächter. Sexualität und Lust im Raum des Heiligen*, Regensburg 1992. See the sources given here on 11-19.
24. The 'Salmonic sound' is an allusion to Salmon, a figure of Greek mythology. He despised the gods and therefore used to travel around the streets of the city in a bronze chariot, dressed as Zeus, imitating thunder and throwing burning torches to mimic lightning.
25. Haug, 'Das Komische und das Heilige' (n.12), 264f.
26. Jacobelli, *Ostergelächter* (n.23), 30f.
27. For the christology of Paul see Kuschel (ed.), *Born Before All Time?* (n.2), 266-307.
28. Gross and Kuschel, 'Ich schaffe Finsternis und Unheil' (Ch.II, n.19).
29. J.Moltmann, *Theology and Joy*, London and New York 1973, 53. For the same complex of questions see G.M.Martin, *Fest und Alltag. Bausteine zu einer Theorie des Festes*, Stuttgart 1973.

IV Learning to Laugh: A Literary and Theological Tableau

1. For Hesse see Kuschel, *'Vielleicht hält Gott sich einige Dichter'* (Ch.III, n.22), Chapter VI, 'Hermann Hesse und die Abgründigkeit der Seele'.
2. H.Hesse, *Steppenwolf*, London 1929, reissued Harmondsworth 1965, 250.
3. H.Hesse, 'Nachwort', in *Materialien zu H.Hesse 'Der Steppenwolf'*, Frankfurt am Main 1972, 159.
4. Hesse, *Steppenwolf* (n.2), 257.
5. Ibid., 66f.
6. Haug, 'Das Komische und das Heilige' (III n.12), 260.
7. K.Tucholsky, 'Kleines Gespräch mit unerwartetem Ausgang', in *Gedichte*, ed. M.Gerold-Tucholsky, Hamburg 1983, 78f.
8. F.Dürrenmatt, 'Theaterprobleme', in id., *Theater-Schriften und Reden*, Zurich 1966, 128.
9. K.Tucholsky, 'Nachher', in *Gesammelte Werke* X, Hamburg 1975, 145.
10. Ibid., 119.
11. Ibid., 140f.
12. S.Freud, *Jokes and their Relation to the Unconscious* (1905), The Penguin Freud Library Vol.6, Harmondsworth 1976. Cf. H.Strozka, 'Witz und Humor', in *Psychologie des 20.Jahrhunderts* II (*Freud und die Folgen* I), ed. D.Eicke, Zurich 1976, 305-21.
13. Freud, *Jokes* (n.12), 163ff.
14. Ibid., 200.
15. This and other Christian jokes are collected in H.von Campenhausen, *Theologenspiess und Spass. Christliche und unchristliche Scherze*, Göttingen ⁷1988, 47.
16. Thus C.Schmid, Introduction to S.Landmann (ed.), *Der jüdische Witz*.

Soziologie und Sammlung, Olten and Freiburg im Breisgau [13]1988, 7-
9: 7.

17. The most representative collection in German is still Landmann (ed.),
Der jüdische Witz (n.16), see 464, 451.

18. Ibid., 13.

19. Ibid., 461.

20. Ibid., 483.

21. E.Bloch, 'Erbschaft dieser Zeit' (1935), Frankfurt am Main 1973, 169;
cf. also id., *The Principle of Hope* (three vols.), Oxford 1986 (Ch.27
'Better Castles in the Air in Fair and Circus, in Fairytale and Colportage').
For the therapeutic function of laughter cf. recently H.Rubinstein,
Lachen macht gesund. Über die Heilkraft von Lachen und Fröhlichkeit,
Landsberg 1987.

22. L.Bechstein, *Märchen*, Stuttgart and Vienna 1992, 184-8: 185. For the
place of the fairy tale in literary history cf. F.Karlinger, *Geschichte des
Märchens im deutschen Sprachraum*, Darmstadt [2]1988.

23. Bechstein, *Märchen*, 187.

24. E.Mörike, 'Die Historie von der schönen Lau', in *Sämtliche Werke*, ed.
H.G.Göpfert, Munich 1964, 936-57: 938.

25. Ibid., 955.

26. For the contemporary background cf. E.Ermatinger, *Gottfried Keller.
Eine Biographie* (1950), Zurich 1990, 444-66. Equally fundamental is
A.Muschg, *Gottfried Keller*, Munich 1977.

27. G.Keller, 'Das verlorene Lachen', in *Sämtliche Werke und ausgewählte
Briefe* II, ed.C.Heselhaus, Munich 1958, 445-530: 449.

28. Ibid., 490.

29. Ibid., 477.

30. Ibid., 497.

31. Ibid., 499.

32. Ibid., 511f.

33. Ibid., 527.

34. B.Neumann, Postscript to *Die Leute von Seldwyla*, Stuttgart 1993, 653-
700: 699.

35. Keller, 'Das verlorene Lachen', 528.

36. Ibid., 529.

37. Ibid., 252.

38. For Kafka see Kuschel, *'Vielleicht hält Gott sich einige Dichter'* (Ch.III,
n.22, Chapter III, 'Franz Kafka und die Unheimlichkeit der Welt'). For
the motif of laughter in Kafka see G.Kranz, 'Kafkas Lachen', in id.,
*Kafkas Lachen und andere Schriften zur Literatur 1950-1990 mit einer
Kranz-Bibliographie* ed. E.Schenkel, Cologne and Vienna 1991, 1-16;
J.Wertheimer, ' "Geflecht aus Narrheit und Schmerz". Lachen und
Überleben bei Kafka im Kontext der jüdischen Tradition', in Vogel (ed.),
Vom Lachen (I, n.4), 45-59.

39. F.Kafka, *Briefe an Felice und andere Korrespondenz aus der Verlo-*

bungszeit, ed.E.Heller and J.Born, Frankfurt am Main 1976, 236-40: 238.

40. Ibid., 239f.
41. There is a wealth of material especially in the fine article by Kranz, 'Kafkas Lachen' (n.38).
42. Bergson, *Laughter* (Introduction n.7), 4, 5.
43. Cf. the extraordinarily illuminating collection by G.Raithel, *Lach, wenn du kannst. Der aggressive Witz von und über Amerikas Minderheiten*, Frankfurt am Main 1975.
44. Thus D.Wellershoff, 'Infantilismus als Revolte oder das ausgeschlagene Erbe – Zur Theorie des Blödelns', in *Das Komische*, ed. W.Preisendanz and R.Warning (I, n.3), 336.
45. The verse comes from Celan's poem 'The Fugue of Death'.
46. There is material on this in H.Läuffer (ed.), *Der Spass ist ein Meister aus Deutschland. Geschichte der guten Laun 1933-1990*, Cologne 1993.
47. H.Boll, *Frankfurter Vorlesungen*, Munich 1968, 114.
48. Ibid., 115.
49. Ibid., 114f.
50. L.Boff, 'Die beiden Sackgassen des Bewahrens und des Erschaffens', in B.Kroeber (ed.), *Zeichen in Umberto Ecos Roman Der Name der Rose*, 347-62: 357 (see I, n.39).
51. Thus M.Thomas, 'Die mystische Elemente und ihre Funktion im Roman *Der Name der Rose*', in Haverkamp and Haidt (eds.), *Ecos Rosenroman* (I, n.39), 123-51, esp. 137-48.
52. G.Wieland, 'Gottes Schweigen und das Lachen der Menschen', in Haverkamp and Haidt (eds.), *Ecos Rosenroman* (I n.39), 97-122: 110.
53. Ibid., 115.
54. Ibid., 116.
55. For Eco's understanding of the 'apocalyptists' cf. U.Eco, *Apocalittici e Integrate: Communicazioni di massa e teorie della cultura di massa*, 1964.
56. H.Kelber, 'Der Autor und sein Roman. Hinführung zu Umberto Ecos *Der Name der Rose*', in Haverkamp and Haidt (eds.), *Ecos Rosenroman* (I, n.39), 56.
57. Ibid, 56f. This is also well put by Wieland: 'William proclaims a simple and entertaining message. In view of the failure of politics, which is concerned only with power and knows no justice; in view of the failure of reason, which proves too weak to cope with reality and therefore only represents interests: those of the powerful or the weak – there remains nothing for human beings than to ward off everything strange, above all excessive claims to absoluteness, by laughter. However, the world of laughter has parted company with ideas of the true, the good, the just; it is a world of resignation and renunciation, tired and old, far removed from the innocent cheerfulness of childish play. William and

his world have left the naiveties of the Enlightenment behind them. Belief in the knowledge of truth and the liberation of human beings from dependences has been lost. What is left is a voluntary aestheticizing of the situation in the world' (120f.).

58. Wittgenstein, *Tractatus* (I, n.67), no.6.41, p.183.
59. L.Wittgenstein, *Notebooks 1914-1916*, Oxford 1961, 74e.
60. Ibid., 72/3e.
61. H.Cox, *The Feast of Fools* (III, 20), 157.

For *further investigation of the specifically theological or literary problems discussed in this book see the following of my publications:*

Systematic theology

Lust an der Erkenntnis – Theologie des 20.Jahrhunderts. Ein Lesebuch, Munich 1986, new edition 1994
Born Before All Time? The Dispute over Christ's Origin, London and New York 1992
'Ich schaffe Finsternis und Unheil' – Ist Gott verantwortlich für das Übel (with Walter Gross), Mainz 1992
Hans Küng, Denkwege – Ein Lesebuch, Munich 1992
Hans Küng. New Horizons of Faith and Thought (with Hermann Häring), London and New York 1993

Ecumenism

Wörterbuch des Christentum (with V.Drehsen, H.Häring and H.Siemers), Gütersloh 1988
Gegenentwürfe – 24 Lebensläufe für eine andere Theologie (with H.Häring), Munich 1988
Leben in ökumenischem Geist – Ein Plädoyer wider die Resignation, Ostfildern 1991

Theological Aesthetics

Jesus in der deutschsprachigen Gegenwartsliteratur, with a preface by Walter Jens, Zürich and Gütersloh 1978, reissued Munich 1987
Stellvertreter Christi? Der Papst in der zeitgenössischen Literatur, Zurich and Gütersloh 1980
Der andere Jesus – Ein Lesebuch moderner literarischer Texte, Zurich and Gütersloh 1987, ²1991

Weil wir uns auf dieser Erde nicht ganz zuhause fühlen – *12 Schriftsteller über Religion und Literatur*, Munich 1985

Theologie und Literatur – Zum Stand des Dialogs (with W.Jens and H.Küng), Munich 1986

Und Maria trat aus ihren Bildern – *Literarische Texte*, Freiburg im Breisgau 1990

Wie kann denn ein Mensch schuldig werden? – *Literarische und theologiche Perspektiven von Schuld* (with Ulrich Baumann), Munich 1990

'Vielleicht hält Gott sich einige Dichter.' Literarisch-theologische Portraits, Mainz 1991

'Ich glaube nicht, dass ich Atheist bin' – *Neue Gespräche über Religion und Literatur*, Munich 1992

World Ecumene

Weltfriede durch Religionsfrieden – Antworten aus den Weltreligionen (with Hans Küng), Munich 1993

Global Ethic. The Declaration of the World's Parliament of Religions (with H.Küng), London and New York 1993

Der Streit um Abraham – Was Juden, Christen und Muslime eint und trennt, Munich 1994

Index